About Island Press

Since 1984, the nonprofit Island Press has been stimulating, shaping, and communicating the ideas that are essential for solving environmental problems worldwide. With more than 800 titles in print and some 40 new releases each year, we are the nation's leading publisher on environmental issues. We identify innovative thinkers and emerging trends in the environmental field. We work with world-renowned experts and authors to develop cross-disciplinary solutions to environmental challenges.

Island Press designs and implements coordinated book publication campaigns in order to communicate our critical messages in print, in person, and online using the latest technologies, programs, and the media. Our goal: to reach targeted audiences—scientists, policymakers, environmental advocates, the media, and concerned citizens—who can and will take action to protect the plants and animals that enrich our world, the ecosystems we need to survive, the water we drink, and the air we breathe.

Island Press gratefully acknowledges the support of its work by the Agua Fund, Inc., The Margaret A. Cargill Foundation, Betsy and Jesse Fink Foundation, The William and Flora Hewlett Foundation, The Kresge Foundation, The Forrest and Frances Lattner Foundation, The Andrew W. Mellon Foundation, The Curtis and Edith Munson Foundation, The Overbrook Foundation, The David and Lucile Packard Foundation, The Summit Foundation, Trust for Architectural Easements, The Winslow Foundation, and other generous donors.

The opinions expressed in this book are those of the author(s) and do not necessarily reflect the views of our donors.

PRINCIPLES OF
BROWNFIELD REGENERATION

PRINCIPLES OF BROWNFIELD REGENERATION

Cleanup, Design, and Reuse of Derelict Land

Justin B. Hollander,
Niall G. Kirkwood, and Julia L. Gold

Washington | Covelo | London

ISLAND PRESS is a trademark of the Center for Resource Economics.

Library of Congress Cataloging-in-Publication Data

Hollander, Justin B.
 Principles of brownfield regeneration : clean up, design, and reuse of derelict land / Justin B. Hollander, Niall G. Kirkwood, and Julia L. Gold.
    p. cm.
 Includes bibliographical references and index.
 ISBN-13: 978-1-59726-722-9 (cloth : alk. paper)
 ISBN-10: 1-59726-722-8 (cloth : alk. paper)
 ISBN-13: 978-1-59726-723-6 (pbk : alk. paper)
 ISBN-10: 1-59726-723-6 (pbk : alk. paper)
 1. Urban renewal—United States—Case studies. 2. City planning—United States. 3. Cities and towns—United States—Growth. 4. Brownfields. I. Kirkwood, Niall. II. Gold, Julia L. III. Title.
 HT175.H65 2010
 307.3′4160973—dc22

                                                                                    2010010288

Printed using Times New Roman

Text design by Karen Wenk
Typesetting by Karen Wenk

Printed on recycled, acid-free paper

Manufactured in the United States of America
10 9 8 7 6 5 4 3 2 1

Keywords: Activity Use Limitation (AUL); Assunpink Creek Greenway, Trenton, NJ; Bioremediation; Community planning; Contaminated land; Eastern Fine Paper project, Brewer, ME; environmental health; infill development; integrated planning, phytoremediation, smart growth, Steel Yards, Providence, RI; stormwater and site drainage, Urban revitalization; Watershed at Hillsdale, Portland, OR

Table of Contents

Chapter 1   Introduction   1

Chapter 2   Approaching Brownfield Redevelopment   7

Chapter 3   Remediation   21

Chapter 4   Land Use and Design Considerations   51

Chapter 5   Case Studies   65

   The Steel Yard, Providence, Rhode Island   68

   Assunpink Greenway, Trenton, New Jersey   80

   June Key Community Center Demonstration Project, Portland,
      Oregon   91

   Eastern Manufacturing Facility, Brewer, Maine   98

   The Watershed at Hillsdale, Portland, Oregon   110

   Additional Resources   121

   Notes   125

   Index   129

Acknowledgments

This book would not have been possible without the essential advice provided by our interviewees and case-study project managers. We would like to recognize them and thank them for their time and willingness to contribute to our research. Their experiences are invaluable and will surely help many other first-timers succeed. We wish them the best of luck as they complete their projects and move on to future ventures.

We would like to thank Barbara Parmenter, from Tufts University, for her advice and editorial support early in the writing of this book. Many thanks also go to Heather Boyer, Courtney Lix, and Sharis Simonian at Island Press for shepherding this project from inception to completion. Finally, we would like to express our deep appreciation to our graduate students who are engaged in brownfield design and planning research and will become the next generation of innovative and engaged practitioners.

CHAPTER 1

Introduction

For a class of properties that are often contaminated, dilapidated, and dangerous to occupy, brownfields have been remarkably popular in this first part of the twenty-first century. As the world has begun to turn a deep shade of green in practically every arena, from lamp design to air travel, the brownfields concept has taken off like few other ideas in the fields of land use and real estate development.

The term *brownfield* originated in the early 1990s when practitioners and researchers saw how emerging regulatory frameworks designed to protect the environment were, as a side effect, inhibiting the reuse, cleanup, and redevelopment of former industrial and commercial sites. These brownfield visionaries reconceptualized vacant lots and abandoned properties; they invented a new term, *brownfield*, to express both the challenges and opportunities that such sites offered.[1]

The U.S. Environmental Protection Agency defines brownfields as idle real property, the development or improvement of which is impaired by real or perceived contamination.[2] It is the contamination (even perceived contamination) that represents the most significant public problem and the greatest barrier to putting idle property back into use. See Box 1.1 for examples of typical brownfield sites.

BOX 1.1

Common Examples of Brownfields

- light-industrial factory sites
- corner gas stations in cities
- dry-cleaning operations and stores
- manufactured gas plants
- metal-plating factories
- electronics manufacturing
- pharmaceutical plants
- chemical manufacturing
- automobile manufacturing
- tannery factory sites
- utility substations
- textile mills
- oil-tank farms
- shunting yards and rail corridors
- municipal buildings with asbestos insulation
- methamphetamine labs
- graveyards and burial grounds
- remote locations of municipal landfills and decommissioned Department of Defense military reservation land, which house, in addition to many of the industrial uses listed above, specialized conditions of munitions storage, firing ranges, and proving grounds

---

WHY SHOULD WE CARE ABOUT BROWNFIELDS?

Juxtaposed against the "greenfield"—composed of farmland, forest, or pasturelands that have never seen development—brownfields offer a more sustainable land-development choice. By taking full advantage of existing infrastructure, cleaning up contamination, and leaving greenfields untouched in their virgin states, brownfields take center stage in a sustainable planning strategy of thwarting sprawl, preserving open space, reducing greenhouse-gas emissions, and reinvesting in urbanized areas

Figure 1.1. Abandoned factories sit within active industry, often set apart from other uses, like the rolling greenfields in the foreground (illustration by Luisa Oliveira).

and their communities. In rapidly urbanizing areas, brownfields—if reused—can host new development and new uses that would otherwise spread throughout undisturbed landscapes far outside urban centers. Brownfields can help balance regional land-development processes, so that fewer virgin greenfields are despoiled and at the same time underutilized land can be regenerated (see Figure 1.1).

Across the fence from boarded-up brownfield sites sit the neighbors, who often suffer from long-term pollution and the stigma effect on property values associated with abandoned property. Reusing these sites brings many benefits to the quality of life in the surrounding neighborhood, such as reduced crime, enhanced local environmental quality, and improved property values.[3] If integrated into a broader strategic planning framework, brownfield reuse can address broader societal challenges of improved energy efficiency; reduced consumption of natural resources; cleaner air, water, and land; and an overall reduced carbon footprint. For those living near a brownfield, reuse and redevelopment can be transformational—particularly for those plagued by a legacy of environmental injustice.[4]

First and foremost, reusing brownfields is good for the property owner, as a successful remediation can go far in limiting an owner's liabilities at a property. Some owners will "mothball" their brownfields in order to hide from legal and environmental responsibilities, but research has shown that such owners are only making things worse for themselves.[5] Working closely with state and federal regulators can increase a property's real-estate value and allow an owner to leverage that value to address environmental liabilities.

For cities and towns, the broader benefits of brownfields reuse are connected to the economic opportunities presented by restoring environmentally damaged land and eliminating the kinds of blight that scare away new business. For cities like New Bedford, Massachusetts, and Trenton, New Jersey, gaining an international reputation as a place to redevelop brownfields has put them on the map and helped them attract a new cadre of businesses and economic activity into their communities.

Addressing brownfields is a critical piece in a broader set of urban planning strategies that are linking local action with global climate change. Research has shown that development of greenfield sites on the exurban fringe is a key contributor to greenhouse gas emissions, energy use, pollution, and natural-resource consumption.[6] Policies that support brownfield reuse effectively reduce barriers to infill development on existing urban lands, thereby relieving development pressure from these greenfield exurban sites. The result is a lighter carbon footprint and a more sustainable pattern of human settlement.

THE CURRENT STATE OF BROWNFIELDS

By most estimates, the number of brownfields is massive—U.S. government estimates put the number of American brownfields at about half a million, and in Asia and Europe the totals may be just as high.[7] Brownfields are found in both cities and towns, in the rural hinterland, and the inner suburbs. Brownfields are suspected to be present on nearly every continent of the globe, with the greatest prevalence in post-industrial zones—places where industry boomed in the nineteenth or twentieth century and has since waned. But not all brownfields are the same. They range in size, extent of contamination, and market value. The simplest example, the gas station with leaking underground tanks, is often the easiest to redevelop. On the other side of the spectrum are the skeletons of industrial dinosaurs, the defunct steel mill complexes or abandoned mines that have widespread and unknown contamination and little market value.[8] Each class of brownfields demands unique treatments in terms of both remediation and planning (see Figure 1.2).

When the concept of brownfields was born, U.S. federal largesse followed, and over the last fifteen years billions have been spent in combined public/private investments in characterizing, remediating, and redeveloping brownfields.[9] But the billions spent have resulted in a mere modicum of success compared to the sea of derelict sites scattered throughout our cities and towns. More work is certainly needed.

Figure 1.2. Example of a brownfields site, behind barbed wire in Chelsea, Massachusetts (photo by Niall Kirkwood).

While the challenges to brownfields reuse abound, there is ample evidence that one big challenge is knowledge—knowledge about how to even get started with a site, knowledge about the ways to characterize and remediate sites, and knowledge about reusing brownfields, dealing with regulatory officials, and potential liabilities. In this book, we attempt to satisfy this knowledge gap by offering a brief, concise, and clear primer on the topic of brownfields. We offer sufficient guidance on basic design and remediation techniques to prepare the reader to be an effective partner in a brownfields reuse project. This book will serve as a foundation for the kind of on-the-job learning that occurs in any new and novel enterprise; it will also provide the reader with some vocabulary and equip the reader to ask the right kinds of questions. Case studies are presented at the end of the book so the reader can see how the concepts introduced here have been applied in practice. And finally, extensive notes and bibliography at the back of the book offer the next steps for those who want to do further research. It is our goal that this book will enable professionals, activists, and ordinary citizens to become more engaged in getting their brownfields back into use, and thus to help their own communities navigate a path to a sustainable future.

CHAPTER 2

Approaching Brownfield Redevelopment

This chapter introduces many of the key factors that are essential to consider when beginning or planning a brownfield redevelopment. By discussing the stakeholders, programs, and technicalities that are important to be aware of, this chapter can serve as a useful starting point when planning for a project. It is vital that each of the issues discussed below is considered carefully and that all the options and available opportunities are understood when getting involved in a brownfield project. It is easy to overlook critical factors when getting started with a site, but the issues that get pushed aside can play a large role in a project's success.

In approaching this section, the authors considered their own experience working on brownfields and realized that being an expert on a topic can sometime cloud one's memory of being a novice. To balance our extensive experience, we reached out to a distinct subgroup within the brownfields world: first-timers. These real-estate, planning, and environmental professionals all had significant professional experience but had never faced a brownfields project. Using a "snowball sampling" approach—we first talked to our contacts, and then talked to their contacts—we ended up with a group of 25 people who had fairly recently been involved in their first brownfields project. The group included local officials, architects, citizen activists, real-estate developers, leaders of non-profits, and business owners. What follows is a distillation of the advice of these first-timers, improved in a few minor ways by the authors' decades' worth of experience in brownfields and rearticulated as a simple three-step plan for approaching brownfield development.

WHAT TO BE AWARE OF BEFORE GETTING STARTED

Before beginning with a project, it is important to have a clear plan. This may sound obvious, but sometimes it can be easy to begin site remediation without fully understanding what the end result will look like. Many first-time brownfield developers explain that it is easy to rush projects, especially when funding is time sensitive. These first-timers stressed the importance of not letting time dictate decision making and of ensuring adequate preparation for each step before jumping into a project. By thinking through the process from the beginning, it is easier to see the bigger picture. Although brownfield projects have the tendency to change and thus require flexibility, it is crucial that every project have a story to present. Having a clear picture of where a project is and where it is headed will help to build a solid foundation for its future.

Once a project enters the planning stages, a number of simultaneous questions emerge:

1) Who will be involved? That is, what agencies, members of the project team, and individuals or groups within the community?
2) How will the team's preliminary plans be communicated to adjacent property owners and to local and state officials, and how will stakeholders' input be considered in rethinking and redesigning the brownfields reuse strategy?
3) What are the relevant support programs and options for cleanup, liability, insurance, and funding? It is important to remember that every case is unique. The following suggestions can help in navigating the process of cleanup, design, and redevelopment, but in the end each project will create its own path.

BOX 2.1

HYPOTHETICAL TEAM

- Lead developer, company, or organization
- Project manager and assistant
- Local, state, and federal agencies
- Environmental engineer
- Environmental attorney
- Environmental consultant
- Architect
- Landscape architect
- Contractor
- Local community groups and non-profits

OTHERS TO INCLUDE

- Grant providers
- Neighborhood residents
- Owners or residents of adjacent properties
- Local politicians
- Neighborhood businesses

STEP 1: FIGURE OUT WHO WILL BE INVOLVED

In most cases, a brownfield redevelopment will include a variety of professionals, agencies, and community members. (See Box 2.1 for a list of hypothetical team members and others who might be involved in a project). It can be difficult to know from the beginning whom to include in plans, conversations, or meetings, but involving the appropriate parties from the beginning is a crucial aspect of brownfield work. Often, individuals or agencies are brought on board in the middle of the process, but this can complicate and slow down a project. By bringing people together from the beginning, it's possible to create a united team where everyone understands the project goals and their own responsibilities.

The first group that should be organized is an on-site team. This can be a large team including many different professionals, or the team can be smaller, depending on the project and its requirements. Involving experienced professionals in this team is one of the most important considerations during a project, especially if other team members have never worked with brownfields. Given the many unique components of brownfield redevelopment, it is crucial to have knowledgeable and experienced people working closely on a project throughout the whole process. Project managers from all over the country said that the need to put together the right team was one of the most important lessons they had learned.

While hiring the right people can be difficult if project managers are unfamiliar with the process, there are many useful resources to help build the best team. Local and state agencies or project managers from other redevelopments can provide information and recommend people with whom they have worked on projects. It can be easy to rush into a project once the process has begun, but taking time on this initial step is crucial. A project must have a team that will help it go smoothly and facilitate its success.

Once a core team has been assembled, project managers must decide which other individuals and groups should be involved in the project or at least be informed of its progress (see Box 2.1). This can be an overwhelming step, especially if there are project details that are still unclear. If the Environmental Protection Agency (EPA) is involved with a project, they may be able to help project managers understand which state and local agencies should be included. Depending on the local regulations, there may be agencies that will have to be involved later in the process. It is best to investigate this and bring these agencies on board from the start. Waiting to involve people or agencies will usually complicate the process and, in some cases, create more work and difficulty as the project moves forward.

There are various ways to involve the different members of a team. Depending on the project and the people involved, it may or may not be necessary for everyone to work closely together. However, projects that have been successful in collaboration and efficiency have had very specific plans about how to do this. In the Watershed case study on page 110, the project's success had to do largely with the coordination and teamwork that characterized each phase of work. As soon as the project was announced, all of the stakeholders were brought together to meet each other and discuss the project. Before construction began, everyone came together to go over the project details and everyone's individual responsibilities. While this process does not sound difficult, it is easy to disregard it when other aspects of a project are moving forward. Unfortunately, projects that struggle are often the ones that do not have a united or structured team of professionals. By making sure everyone working on a project knows their responsibilities, as well as everyone else's, the group can succeed as a team.

STEP 2: CREATE A COMMUNITY OUTREACH PLAN

In addition to bringing together all the professionals involved in a project, it is necessary to have a community outreach plan. Engaging and informing the community from the start of a project is crucial. People want to know what is happening in their neighborhood and all outreach should be done with care. Depending on the site, the community may or may not be involved. However, they should be given a chance to learn what is going on and to present their questions or concerns. This is usually done in community meetings, but larger projects will also incorporate other techniques to inform their communities.

The Assunpink Creek Greenway project on page 80 included an outside group in their project to help with informing and engaging the community of Trenton, New Jersey. Because of the extended time frame and the large scale of the project, a collaborative of nonprofits joined together to serve as the liaison between the city of Trenton (the project manager) and the local residents. This has been extremely successful and has helped the city to give a neutral perspective to its residents and keep them up to date over the many years the project has been in progress. The Assunpink Creek Greenway and many other project teams have recognized the value of involving any interested individuals and giving them opportunities to share their questions and comments. A project that does this well will see greater community support and long-term involvement. But if this is done poorly, the community may never be willing to fully support the project. Not only can this delay a project's completion, it may also affect the overall success of a project after it is completed. When the community is involved in a project from the beginning, its members can serve as team players. Whether or not they are actively involved, they will feel more comfortable if they are informed and will consider themselves a part of the work that is being done.

STEP 3: FIND RESOURCES AND SUPPORT SERVICES

There is nothing ordinary about reusing a brownfields site, so the ordinary support services available for development tend to be insufficient for brownfields. Additional and highly specialized resources and support services are needed for a brownfields project to succeed. The place to start is at the top: federal brownfields programs. These federal resources are the largest sources for support for most projects, and they also serve as a point of entry connecting brownfields developers with the broad array of state, local, legal, and insurance programs available.

Federal Brownfields Programs

In advance of a new project, the vast world of federal policy, regulation, and funding can seem daunting. A veritable alphabet soup of federal agencies are concerned with brownfields projects, in some cases all at the same time! With respect to environmental investigation and remediation, the U.S. EPA can be an important source of funding, technical assistance, and best practices in any brownfields project. Depending on the environmental conditions at a site, the EPA may also play a role in regulating the investigation and remediation process—however, in most cases state environmental agencies play that role.[1] Through the EPA's network of regional field offices and its headquarters staff, the agency provides guidance and support to brownfields developers—primarily through resources posted to its website <www.epa.gov/brownfields>.

Most other federal agencies get involved in brownfields by supporting redevelopment after preliminary environmental investigation has been completed. The Department of Housing and Urban Development (HUD), the Economic Development Administration (EDA), the Department of Energy (DOE), the National Oceanic and Atmospheric Agency (NOAA), and the EPA all provide grants, low-interest loans, and direct technical support to local government agencies to aid in building new structures or other uses on brownfields.

These myriad programs are in a constant state of flux, but a few constants over the years are worth noting. The EPA's Brownfields Program has been providing grants and loans for both the cleanup and reuse of brownfields since 1996. These grants and loans are offered on a competitive basis and they primarily fund environmental assessment and planning, but the program has recently evolved to support more remediation and reuse. The EPA's program has pumped more than $100 million into brownfields projects and is widely viewed as a successful policy intervention.[2]

Equally important for local governments for at least a decade has been the use of HUD's Community Development Block Grant (CDBG) program to fund brownfield projects.[3] While individual communities have had mixed success with using CDBG monies to fund brownfields, in general the program has been flexible enough to help cover some of the costs for hundreds of projects across the country. And the use of CDBG funds for brownfields only looks like it will increase under the Obama Administration, with the signing of an interagency Partnership for Sustainable Communities on June 16, 2009, between HUD, EPA, and the Department of Transportation, to support a coordinated approach to promoting, among other things, "land recycling."[4]

State Brownfields Programs

Following the lead of the EPA in the mid-1990s, many U.S. states developed their own versions of a grant-making and technical assistance program for brownfields. While the most aggressive of these programs are geographically concentrated in the Northeast and Midwest, states across the Sunbelt, such as California, Florida, and Virginia, also have well-funded and robust programs. Even in states that do not have formal brownfields programs in place, such as North Dakota, there are still regulatory and economic-development policies in place that can support brownfields projects—even if that is not the intended purpose of the regulations or policies.

It is in states with strong programs, such as New Jersey, Pennsylvania, and Ohio, where state agencies have played a critical role in streamlining environmental reviews for brownfields, offsetting costs associated with remediation, and subsidizing redevelopment costs.[5] For these active states, professionals trained in brownfields investigation, reuse, and redevelopment often serve as project managers for regulatory agencies with the express purpose of helping to make projects happen. This is in stark contrast to states where environmental regulators sit in a stovepipe organization with little real interest in the end use of sites. This lack of focus on future use of a property can delay reuse for years or decades due to ongoing environmental review and remediation.

Policy innovators in New Jersey responded to this challenge in the early 2000s by adopting an alternate route for environmental review using a field-based approach to investigation called Triad. Under Triad, decisions about contamination levels and remediation strategies are made in the field in real time by regulators working in close communication with property owners. Triad offers a potentially powerful approach to reducing both the time needed in negotiations as well as delays related to investigation.

A second important innovation at the state level is the use of environmental consultants in place of government employees in the assessment and evaluation of site conditions as part of the normal regulatory review process. These Licensed Site Professionals (LSP) or Licensed Environmental Professionals (LEP) as they are called in some states, undergo extensive training and must meet certain minimum educational requirements, including specialization in hydrology, geology, hydrogeology, soil science, or environmental engineering.

LSP programs have allowed the limited personnel, resources, and expertise of state environmental regulation and enforcement offices to be augmented by a privatized system of professional consultants. These professionals help to move the ever-growing backlog of brownfield site evaluations and responses to ensure these sites are returned to a higher and better use in a timely manner. They are hired to work in consultation with federal and state regulators, local officials, planners, and designers to assess and evaluate the environmental conditions of sites (technical and regulatory), assist site owners in understanding site conditions and the site owners' obligations regarding compliance, and to devise appropriate remediation, reuse, and monitoring strategies to be used. It is likely LSPs will work on a brownfield project with clients who either own sites or are involved in transactions to purchase them—that is, attorneys, regulators, lenders and banks, site contractors, municipalities, local stakeholders, and other environmental professionals.

For those initiating a brownfields project in a state with LSPs, there may be significant cost and time benefits, but not all states have jumped on this bandwagon.[6]

Local Government Considerations

The state and federal context is critical to approaching a brownfield project, but it is at the local level where a project's feasibility is really tested. Local politics matters most in any brownfield project and the ability of a project team to navigate a neighborhood's power structure is essential. While local regulatory authority rarely extends to governing the investigation or remediation of brownfields, in most states, localities exert strong controls over the ultimate reuse or redevelopment of a site. Additionally, local governments can (with state approval) offer great flexibility with respect to taxation for a brownfields project, funnel federal and state monies to projects, help with off-site infrastructure, and assist with site assembly by invoking eminent domain.[7]

A recent favorite policy tool for local brownfields redevelopment has been Tax Increment Financing, a mechanism that allows cities and towns to borrow money with the aim of paying it back with the increased taxes that an economic development project is intended to generate.[8] The borrowed money can pay for infrastructure related to a project or can even assist with redevelopment costs. Local governments can also delay or reduce property taxes for brownfields developers as an incentive to make projects happen. As a project draws on federal, state, and private resources, such local support can fill in the final funding gaps. The best place to start is with town or city officials where a brownfield is located. A brownfields coordinator is an ideal first point of contact for information, but not all cities and towns have someone in such a position. Otherwise, it is best to reach out to city planners who are knowledgeable about federal and state programs.

Legal Liability and Insurance Considerations

Liability is the single most important concept to understand in approaching a brownfield project. The very reason that so many brownfields exist is that property owners are too concerned about the risk of legal liability they may be exposed to when they own contaminated property. The federal laws known as CERCLA, introduced in 1980, were viewed as too harsh in establishing liability for contamination to anyone in the chain of title—that is, anyone who ever owned a contaminated property outright, held a mortgage for such a property, or even maintained an easement through a such a property.[9] This draconian policy had a chilling effect on the industrial real-estate market, and only in 2002 did this begin to change as CERCLA was amended to limit liability to those parties who had a direct connection to perpetrating the contamination.[10]

Today, the question of liability remains a critical one and demands the attention of a lawyer trained in environment risks. For a site with major contamination, a project developer must be aware of the liability she might assume if her remediation efforts are not done correctly. Mistakes and errors in remediation can cause greater pollution and can saddle a project developer with further liability. With proper counsel, a site can be investigated, remediated, and redeveloped without the project developer incurring any further liability—it can be done, but should not be taken lightly.

One of the most significant mechanisms developed to protect the past owner from continued liability related to contamination is for future use of the property to be restricted. The legal mechanism used is known as an Activity Use Limitation (AUL) and is inserted as a covenant into the transfer deed for a brownfields property. The AUL is often negotiated between the property owner and the state or federal regulatory agency with oversight responsibility; it seeks to protect human health and the environment, while making the property available for a limited range of uses.

The most common type of AUL restricts properties with some residual contamination to commercial or industrial uses, prohibiting residential or day-care uses. AULs also can be written to cover only portions of a site, thereby allowing day-care facilities on part of the site, or housing on part of the site, but prohibiting anyone except workers wearing full-body protection from other parts of a site. In many ways, the AUL has been a valuable tool in getting brownfields into reuse, protecting owners' liability, and most important, protecting people from exposure to toxic environments.

The insurance industry has tentatively entered the brownfields arena by offering several products intended to protect project developers both from liability associated with their remediation (pollution liability policies) and from long-term costs related to unknown environmental problems at a site (cleanup cost-cap policies). While such policies are not inexpensive, nor are they easy to secure, they can be useful for building consensus among local officials, regulators, project developers, and other stakeholders. This kind of insurance provides some level of assurance that a site will be cleaned, that the project developers will not be financially ruined by the endeavor, and that future, unknown contaminants will be addressed.

To learn more about insurance or liability related to a brownfields site, the best first stop is <www.brownfieldsinsurance.org>, a website sponsored by the U.S. EPA. There, one can search for legal counsel and insurance providers and peruse a library of reports, case studies, and articles about insurance and liability surrounding brownfields. Laws governing environmental responsibility and remediation standards are constantly changing and vary from state to state, so it is best to consult a

real-estate lawyer with experience in dealing with contaminated properties before making any decisions about insurance.

GOING THE NEXT STEP: TOWARD REMEDIATION

While there are many factors to consider in a successful brownfield redevelopment project, the three-step plan described in this chapter can help
any project succeed. In addition to these lessons that have come from
first-time brownfield developers, it is important to search for additional
advice throughout the duration of a project. Networking with other project teams can be an effective way to learn about new techniques or programs and to receive support and advice from others doing similar work.
A good place to start is to reach out to a local brownfields coordinator in
your city or town. If your local government does not have someone in
that capacity, then talk to the state, provincial, or federal brownfields officials who cover your territory. Each of these government agencies hosts

---

BOX 2.2

Electronic Resources for Those New to Brownfields

U.S. Environmental Protection Agency's Brownfields Office
    www.epa.gov/brownfields
The Brownfields and Land Revitalization Technology Support Center
    www.brownfieldstsc.org/
The National Center for Neighborhood and Brownfields Redevelopment
    policy.rutgers.edu/brownfields/
Western Pennsylvania Brownfields Center
    www.cmu.edu/steinbrenner/brownfields/index.html
West Virginia Brownfields Assistance Center
    www.wvbrownfields.com
National Brownfields Association
    www.brownfieldassociation.org/

websites (some better than others) that provide various resources and toolkits to aid first-timers. (See Box 2.2 for a list of online resources.)

The three-step plan introduced here will get a brownfields project started. After preliminary work is complete, a much thornier stage of environmental investigation and remediation follows. In the next chapter, we introduce the process of studying the environmental conditions of a site and provide an introduction to the range of contaminants that may be encountered as well as various available strategies for remediating those contaminants.

CHAPTER 3

Remediation

There are a number of factors to consider in this phase of the cleanup of a brownfield site. The most significant are the relevant cleanup standard(s) and the method(s) selected to reach the standard(s). The standards arise from an assessment of the risk to human and environmental receptors and the published maximum detectable limits allowable as established by the federal government (the United States Environmental Protection Agency—U.S. EPA) and state agencies (Departments of Environment) for each contaminant type. This information is available on federal or state agency websites or through their many publications available online.

An environmental engineer or licensed site professional (LSP) will carry out a thorough analysis of the existing site conditions and relevant environmental factors. Following the analysis, a remediation plan will be drawn up by the environmental engineer or LSP that outlines the most effective and expedient method of addressing the environmental contamination on-site to render the site safe for reuse, with no significant risk (see Figure 3.1). This has tended to be a "one-size-fits-all" approach where a site is entirely remediated irrespective of the final end use, causing in many cases unneeded expense and disruption. More recently, federal and state regulatory agencies have approved risk-based assessment of brownfields that tailors remedial action to the planned end use of sites. Site programs and uses vary in their need for reduction of contamination sources, from light industrial, which can require minimal intervention, to day-care centers, schools, and senior housing at the other end of the scale that can require extensive remediation measures to be taken.

Remedial action can range from the removal of a modest amount of soil, with limited disturbance to the site and its eventual redevelopment, to large-scale engineering works that demolish derelict buildings and remove all of the site's soils and water bodies. One significant issue regarding brownfields remediation is that more than one pollutant is usually found on the site in soils and groundwater. In reality, the simple idea of

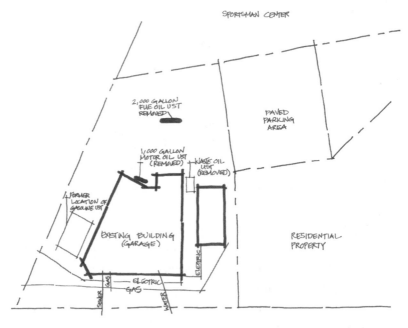

Figure 3.1. Site diagram illustrating an Environmental Site Investigation for brownfields (illustration by Luisa Oliveira).

one on-site pollutant with one remediation technology to address it is replaced by multiple pollutants found in many locations in various conditions and mixed together as a "cocktail" of contaminants on-site. In addition, certain small areas or "hotspots" may have intense chemical concentrations requiring immediate treatment. This requires the remediation process to be considered as a "train" of technologies, assembled over time by the licensed site professional, that address a multiple range of pollutants.

How Contaminated Is a Site?

Brownfields are predominantly found in urban or exurban areas adjacent to or within industrial, commercial, or residential neighborhoods. Examples of typical settings include the following:

- *isolated landfill sites* close to or within the boundaries of towns, cities, and communities
- *part of the built urban fabric* adjacent to port-lands, docks, harbors, railroad yards and corridors, riverfronts, airfields, and industrial manufacturing districts
- *isolated brownfield sites* in suburban and rural areas where industrial, manufacturing, or polluting agricultural practices have occurred or are still carried out
- *specialized brownfields* located on former Department of Defense facilities, as well as mining and extraction sites usually at some distance from built-up areas

The following are some of the most common elements of a brownfield site:

- abandoned or semi-abandoned, padlocked, rusted, and potentially structurally hazardous industrial building structures set within an external landscape of broken asphalt and stained concrete slabs

- mounds of toxic and non-toxic industrial waste, lagoons, ponds, pools, and canals with standing water and bottom sediments and sludge
- underground and surface oil tanks and storage vats
- above- and below-ground infrastructure, including transformers, sewage and sanitation chambers, pipe ducts, utility corridors, overhead ducts, industrial equipment, barrels, and debris produced within or brought to and disposed of on-site
- infrastructure of rail corridors and roads, including signals and tracks, catch basins, storage pits and road beds

Due to the lack of human presence, these sites may also contain a diversity of pioneer adaptive urban wildlife, insect, and plant communities. These sites provide rich and varied habitats within city neighborhoods and, as such, have great value despite their contaminated conditions. However, any determination of the presence of contamination, or lack thereof, has to go beyond the apparent degraded visual and aesthetic conditions to determine the extent of potential pollutants to be found:

- in the ground-surface soils of the site
- in the standing and subsurface groundwater
- in sediments found in tanks, pools, ponds, rivers, and canals
- in the physical materials of the building construction
- within site infrastructure, catch basins, ducts, and pipe-work channels
- in on-site civil engineering works
- as part of indoor and outdoor air studies

Traditional forms of site analysis currently employed by site designers for any type of site (greenfield, greyfield, etc.) focus on issues such as access and circulation, existing and proposed utilities, topography, microclimate, existing vegetation and building structures, site stability, and drainage, as well as the pH, organic content, and structure of the soil. Initial evaluation of brownfield sites requires the analysis of a broader set of environmental and planning/design criteria focused on the potential pollutants.

Many of the contaminants can be found in on-site built or natural infrastructure, including

- fuel-storage bunkers
- lagoons
- pools
- cooling ponds
- canals
- dock wharves
- railroad tracks and ties
- waste slag/storage fields
- catch basins and drains

In addition, vegetation (both native and introduced) and water bodies have to be considered as part of the overall environmental and ecological understanding and evaluation of the site. Included in this overall understanding are

- adjacent urban river and waterways
- coastal land
- wetlands and swamps
- remnant woodlands
- metro forests

Soils

The occupation of sites for industrial purposes over lengthy periods of time can produce soils that are severely impacted by

- compaction by buildings, roadways, and parking
- waste dumping or burial of industrial waste in shallow pits
- movement of subsurface contamination plumes
- pollutants brought to site over time and mixed in with existing rubble and urban fill

In many cases, the on-site soils lie hidden under existing concrete surfaces or infrastructure and may not come to light until demolition is carried out. A "cocktail" of contaminants can be found at varying depths, ranging from metals in the top 18 inches to depths as extreme as 50 to 60 feet, where waste from former manufacturing processes such as textiles and steel production can be found along with coal ash and wood debris from domestic fires and industrial boilers.

Ground Water

The movement and conditions of ground water on brownfields are likely to be affected by subsurface contamination plumes arising from direct spills or discharges from manufacturing processes on-site or off-site leaks or former illegal disposal of waste streams, industrial by-products in the ground, site drains, swales or soak-aways. In addition, polluted ground water can indicate long-standing problems arising from slow leaking oil-storage tanks buried in the ground. The dynamic nature of subsurface water conditions produces complex flows into and within the site area, and emanating from the site to adjoining lands and local natural resources, including rivers and lakes.

Surface Water

Ponds, pools, and lagoons are commonly found on industrial sites as part of former storage facilities and manufacturing processes. These constructed water bodies are likely to accumulate significant amounts of discharge and surface pollutants from pipeline sources and overflows. In addition, local standing water on sites can indicate previous discharges from buildings or leaking containers.

Sediments

Closely related to surface-water areas, sediments are found at the bottom of tanks, ponds, and pools. These areas of water and sediment can act as reservoirs of contamination that often go unnoticed. Sludge and potentially polluted sediment layers, though spatially contained, pose special cleanup issues due to the accumulated concentrations of contaminants. Their removal is usually necessary either on-site or off-site, although in certain cases encapsulation can leave them undisturbed.

Existing Infrastructure

Buildings found on a brownfield site can range from abandoned, partly derelict, or individual freestanding structures that often require immediate demolition, to larger collections of stone or brick factory structures that may be in various stages of abandonment or dilapidation, yet may be rehabilitated, repaired, and reused. The possible effects of these structures on the site include their continued deterioration if not addressed, as well as the presence of contaminated floors, walls, and architectural materials and finishes (asbestos tile and insulation, lead piping and lead paint) that continue to harbor contaminants that may pollute the larger site area.

The remaining elements or fragments of former industrial processes—cranes, overhead gantries, rails, and freestanding structures, as well as remnants of transportation and circulation systems such as canals, rail platforms, bridges, and walkways—may continue to harbor localized areas of contamination.

Indoor and Outdoor Air

While often overlooked in the site evaluation of brownfields, both indoor and outdoor air can be a potential source of pollution. Gases can be emitted from subsurface tanks and below-grade plumes and pollutants. These gases are then transported in the air into, across, and away from adjacent sites. Potential future contamination from gases and rising vapors underground should be taken into account during the evaluation period.

The following are typical environmental hazards found on brownfield sites:

- volatile organic compounds (VOCs)—for example, solvents and gasoline
- semi-volatile organic compounds (SVOCs)—for example, dyes

- petroleum products (total petroleum hydrocarbons—TPHs)
- pesticides/herbicides
- polychlorinated biphenols (PCBs)
- metals

VOLATILE ORGANIC COMPOUNDS (VOCs)

Volatile Organic Compounds (VOCs) are synthetic organic chemicals that have a high vapor pressure and easily form vapors at normal temperature and pressure. The term is generally applied to organic solvents, certain paint additives, aerosol spray-can propellants, fuels (such as gasoline and kerosene), petroleum distillates, dry-cleaning products, and other industrial and consumer products ranging from office supplies to building materials. VOCs are also naturally emitted by a number of plants and trees. Most VOCs evaporate easily but are not appreciably soluble in water. This class of chemicals covers a wide range of compounds, including toluene, styrene, and many chlorinated solvents found on brownfield sites once occupied by businesses such as printers and engravers, metal finishers, furniture refinishers and auto body shops. VOCs can have direct adverse effects on human health, and many have been classified as toxic and carcinogenic.

SEMI-VOLATILE ORGANIC COMPOUNDS (SVOCs)

Semi-organic volatile compounds (SVOCs) are synthetic organic compounds that are solvent-extractable. They include

- phenols
- phthalates
- polycyclic aromatic hydrocarbons (PAHs) produced during combustion

PETROLEUM PRODUCTS (TPH)

Total petroleum hydrocarbons found on brownfield sites include

- heating oil (from spills or ruptured underground tanks)
- gasoline (from spills and discharges)

- kerosene
- asphalt

PESTICIDES / HERBICIDES

Pesticides are chemicals or mixtures of chemicals used for the prevention, elimination, or control of unwanted insects, plants, and animals. Pesticides are usually organic chemicals but may also be inorganic compounds. They can be produced in the laboratory or may be produced naturally by plants. Herbicides are commonly found in brownfield sites along railroad tracks, rights of way, and rail yards.

POLYCHLORINATED BIPHENYLS (PCBs)

Polychlorinated biphenyls are a class of chemicals known as PCBs. They are entirely man-made and were first manufactured commercially in 1929 in the United States. They are used in many different types of products, including hydraulic fluid, casting wax, pigments, carbonless copy paper, plasticizer, vacum pumps, compressors, and heat transfer systems. Their primary use, however, is as a dielectric fluid in electrical equipment. Because of their stability and resistance to thermal breakdown, as well as their insulating properties, they were the fluid of choice as a transformer and capacitor coolant. PCBs are a suspected human carcinogen and a known animal carcinogen. They are resistant to degradation and therefore persist for many years in the environment. Furthermore, they bioaccumulate in the food chain and are stored in the body fat of animals and humans. PCB contamination from historic uses and dumping is widespread, and it is commonly found on brownfield sites where manufacturing processes have taken place.

METALS

Metals or heavy metals are any metallic chemical elements that have a relatively high density, are highly toxic, and poisonous to humans at low concentrations. Common environmental metal hazards that can cause serious health effects, if there is sufficient exposure, include the following:

- arsenic
- beryllium
- cadmium
- chromium
- nickel
- lead
- zinc
- mercury
- copper

Of all these metals, lead, a naturally occurring substance, is most commonly found on urban brownfield sites. It was used in household and industrial paints, brake pads, and gasoline until it was found to cause learning and behavioral problems in humans, but it is still often found in discarded or buried lead batteries. Lead is neurotoxic, so children whose bodies are still developing are most at risk. While some aspects of lead poisoning are reversible in adults, in children it can interfere with normal development, cause irreparable brain damage, or even result in death. It is therefore extremely important to address the presence of lead in soils on brownfield sites.

TECHNIQUES USED IN REMEDIATION

Remediation technologies are environmental-cleanup solutions for contaminated soils and groundwater, and the technologies used in a remediation plan can be extensive in number and broad in range. Remediation categories are defined by the acceptance of the remediation technology by regulatory authorities and performance results in the field. Finally, the selection of a remediation approach or approaches establishes the extent of environmental cleanup that is proposed. A wide range of remediation technologies are available for cleaning up pollutants found at a brownfield site. Three main categories of remediation technologies are

1. *Established treatment technologies* for which costs and other performance information is readily available.

2. *Innovative alternative-treatment technologies* whose routine use on brownfields are inhibited by lack of data on performance and cost. Currently, they have limited full-scale application.

3. *Emerging alternative-treatment technologies* whose routine use on remediation sites is inhibited by lack of data and evaluation of claims. They are currently found in laboratory test plots and in full-scale pilot-site testing.

An alphabetical list of common remediation technologies now follows to demonstrate the range and type of remediation technologies available to the development team.

Air Sparging

ESTABLISHED TREATMENT TECHNOLOGY

Sparging is the process of injecting air directly into severely polluted groundwater to remediate it by volatilizing or driving off contaminants and enhancing the biodegradation processes. As the injected air bubbles rise in the groundwater, the contaminants are stripped from the groundwater by physical contact with the air and are carried up into the soil, where an extraction fan system is usually used to remove vapors. Owing to the intensive use of apparatus required on-site, air sparging is best suited to situations where removal of a maximum quantity of pollutants from groundwater can be made.

Bioremediation

INNOVATIVE ALTERNATIVE-TREATMENT TECHNOLOGY

Bioremediation is the use of biological agents, such as microbes or plants, to remove or neutralize contaminants in polluted soil or water. Bacteria and fungi need nutrients (such as carbon, nitrogen, phosphate, and trace metals) to survive. They break down organic (carbon-containing) compounds found in nature to get energy for growth. For example, soil bacteria use petroleum hydrocarbons found on brownfield sites as a food and energy source, changing them into relatively harmless substances— carbon dioxide, water, and fatty acids. In some cases microbes already living in the ground on a contaminated site will be used, or new microbes will be injected into the ground. Bioremediation can be used on a variety of organic compounds and are a non-intrusive sustainable method of site cleanup. However, the technology needs time to work and may not be appropriate for brownfields where immediate remedial action is required.

Bioventing

ESTABLISHED TREATMENT TECHNOLOGY

Bioventing is an *in situ* soil treatment technology that involves stimulating the natural biodegradation of petroleum hydrocarbons in soil. During bioventing, the oxygen concentration in the soil gas is increased by injecting air into the contaminated zone through drilled wells. In a few cases some air-extraction wells may be used to control vapor migration. In contrast to soil vapor extraction during air sparging, bioventing uses low airflow rates to provide only enough oxygen to sustain microbial activity. Oxygen is most commonly supplied by directing airflow through residual contamination in soil.

Encapsulation

ESTABLISHED TREATMENT TECHNOLOGY

Encapsulation or "capping" refers to the installation of a cover of soil, clay layer, or a durable waterproof membrane or a combination of them over contaminated material on site. The contaminated materials are left in the ground or can also be placed in a trench lined with a durable waterproof or clay membrane, and the cap prevents human or environmental contact. Encapsulation is appropriate for all levels of polluted soil found on brownfields.

Excavation

ESTABLISHED TREATMENT TECHNOLOGY

Excavation is the isolation, digging up and removal of contaminated soil on-site. The soil is usually excavated with construction equipment such as a backhoe or bulldozer. The soil is then either cleaned or removed from the site and disposed of in an approved landfill. Often the space left open is then filled with clean soil or fill or regraded as part of a site design strategy.

Incineration

ESTABLISHED TREATMENT TECHNOLOGY

Incineration is the process of burning hazardous materials such as polluted soil at a controlled temperature high enough to destroy harmful chemicals. An incinerator can be brought to the cleanup site, or the material can be trucked from the site to an incinerator. The material is placed in the incinerator, where it is intensely heated. To increase the amount of harmful chemicals destroyed, the amount of heat and air is controlled. As the chemicals heat up, they change into gases, which pass through a flame to be heated further. The gases become so hot that they combine with oxygen and break down to form less-harmful gases and steam. These gases then pass through air-pollution-control equipment to remove any remaining metals, acids, and particles of ash. This waste product is harmful and must be properly disposed of in a licensed landfill.

Landfarming

EMERGING ALTERNATIVE-TREATMENT TECHNOLOGY

Land farming is a bioremediation treatment process that is performed in the upper soil zone or in biotreatment cells. Contaminated soils, sediments, or sludges are incorporated into the soil surface and periodically turned over or tilled to aerate the mixture.

Natural Attenuation

INNOVATIVE ALTERNATIVE-TREATMENT TECHNOLOGY

Natural attenuation relies on natural processes to clean up or attenuate pollution in soil and groundwater. Natural attenuation occurs at most polluted sites. However, the right conditions must exist underground to clean sites properly. If not, cleanup will not be quick enough or complete enough. Attenuation comprises a range of subsurface processes, such as dilution, volatilization, biodegradation, adsorption, and chemical reactions with subsurface materials that are allowed to naturally reduce contaminant concentrations to acceptable levels.

Permeable Reactive Barrier

ESTABLISHED TREATMENT TECHNOLOGY

Permeable reactive barriers are walls built below ground to treat contaminated groundwater. The walls are installed across the flow path of a contaminant plume, allowing the water portion of the plume to move passively through the wall. These barriers allow the passage of water while prohibiting the movement of contaminants by employing such agents as zero-valent metals, chelators, sorbents, and microbes that are inserted into the wall in prepared barrier panels. The contaminants will either be degraded or retained in a concentrated form by the barrier material. The wall could provide permanent containment for relatively benign residues or provide a decreased volume of the more toxic contaminants for subsequent treatment.

Phytoremediation

EMERGING ALTERNATIVE-TREATMENT TECHNOLOGY

Phytoremediation is the direct use of living plants to remove or neutralize site contaminants such as heavy metals and organic pollutants found in soils, ground water, or sediments. A more general term, "phytotechnologies," describes a range of plant-based applications that use

Figure 3.2. Site of phytoremediation demonstration program, Trenton, New Jersey (photo by Justin Hollander).

mechanisms in living vegetation to remove, degrade, or contain contaminants. This technology can be used on brownfield sites where a longer time period is available for remediation and if all appropriate growing conditions exist in terms of soil fertility, pH, drainage, water supply, and microclimate (see Figure 3.2).

Pump and Treat

ESTABLISHED TREATMENT TECHNOLOGY

In pump-and-treat systems, groundwater is pumped from below ground to the surface. Once it has been removed from the ground, it is cleaned to remove harmful chemicals and then returned to the ground.

Soil Washing

INNOVATIVE ALTERNATIVE-TREATMENT TECHNOLOGY

Soil washing "scrubs" soil to remove and separate the portion of the soil that is not polluted. This reduces the amount of soil needing further cleanup. The soil-washing process separates the contaminated fine soil (silt and clay) from the coarse soil (sand and gravel). When completed, the smaller volume of soil, which contains the majority of the fine silt and clay particles, can be further treated by other methods (such as incineration or bioremediation) or disposed of according to state and federal regulations. The clean, larger volume of soil is not toxic and can be used as backfill.

Soil Vapor Extraction

ESTABLISHED TREATMENT TECHNOLOGY

Soil vapor extraction (SVE) is an *in situ* process for soil remediation where contamination is removed from soil by passing it out through a medium such as air or steam. Chemicals in soil and groundwater evaporate to form a gas or vapor. In the ground, these vapors can be removed from the soil above the water table by applying a vacuum to pull them out. The extracted soil vapors are separated into liquids and vapors, and each stream is treated as necessary. The basic system used to accomplish this consists of a vapor extraction well, which extends from the surface down to a depth where the soil is contaminated, coupled with blowers or vacuum pumps, which draw air through the contaminated soil up to the surface via the well.

Thermal Desorption

INNOVATIVE ALTERNATIVE-TREATMENT TECHNOLOGY

Thermal desorption utilizes heat to increase the volatility of soil contaminants such that they can be removed (separated) from the solid soil matrix. Unlike an incinerator that destroys by heat and burning, the volatilized contaminants are either collected or thermally destroyed by being broken down chemically. A thermal desorption system therefore has two major components; the desorber itself and the off-gas treatment system. The desorbers are fired rotary systems that use an inclined rotating metallic cylinder to heat the feed material. The heat-transfer mechanism is usually conduction through the cylinder wall. In this type of system neither the flame nor the products of combustion can contact the feed solids or the off-gas. The volatilized contaminants in the off-gas can be collected, destroyed, or discharged to the atmosphere. In some cases, both a collection and destruction system are employed.

The evaluation and selection of these remediation technologies are based on the following criteria:

- ability to protect human health and the environment
- compliance with environmental statutes
- type of contamination to be addressed
- long-term effectiveness and permanence
- reduction of toxicity, mobility, and volume
- short-term effectiveness
- cost
- ability to be implemented
- state acceptance
- community acceptance

Remediation equipment and supporting facilities, including project offices, portable testing laboratories, and protective storage and cleaning areas for workers, can have a significant presence on the site, as can permanent remediation treatments such as pump-and-treatment facilities and their protective buildings, which may be in place for up to fifty years.

ORGANIZING AND ASSESSING THE REMEDIATION EFFORT

Five general approaches to remediation are commonly found. These range from the most intrusive on-site to the least intrusive: full cleanup, partial cleanup (off-site), partial cleanup (in place), full concealment, and nonintrusive cleanup, each to be determined by the environmental site professional. The approach is selected according to the levels, extent, and concentrations of contamination on the brownfield site; the size, location, and physical site working conditions in terms of adjoining stake-holders; the presence of homes close to the working remediation area; and degree of access to the site for equipment and the removal of contaminated material.

Full Cleanup

Full or total cleanup includes complete soil excavation over the entire site and removal by truck to a licensed landfill. In addition a complete dewatering and removal of on-site water bodies (ponds, pools, and lagoons) will be carried out, including cleaning up and removal of any remaining sediment layers. Finally the extraction and removal or remediation of polluted groundwater plumes will be carried out over the whole site area. An example of total cleanup occurs on former gas station sites where, after excavation and removal of the underground storage tanks, the remaining soil is stripped off and trucked off-site.

Partial Cleanup (Off-Site)

Partial cleanup that takes place off-site from a brownfield location is defined by the removal of contaminated soils to another site where the soils will be remediated. This involves handling and transportation by truck of the contaminated material a number of times. Once the material has arrived at the remote location it is treated by one or more of a number of remediation technologies. The final destination of the formerly contaminated soils can be a licensed landfill or another site. Or the soil can be returned to the original brownfield site once it has been cleaned. An advantage of this approach is that the soils of a large number of brownfield sites can be remediated in sequential batches, operating at a city or regional level. Multiple batching results in economies of scale, a specialized labor force, and the efficient use of equipment. Disadvantages include extra costs for haulage and double handling, the need for precise timing of soil removal and deliveries, and the availability of a constant supply of contaminated soils. The remediation technologies that are used off-site include physical methods such as mass incineration and thermal desorption, chemical methods such as soil washing, and biological methods such as land farming and phytoremediation.

Partial Cleanup (In Place)

Partial cleanup in place or *in situ* addresses pollutants where they occur on the brownfield site. This requires remediation technologies and supporting equipment to be brought on-site and the ground surface and excavations to be prepared around other site construction activities. The advantage of *in situ* partial cleanup is the ability to remove the known limits of the pollutants without causing the spread of further contamination. This method makes it possible to isolate different types of pollutants on-site and to apply the precise remediation technology for the contaminant. The disadvantages can include limited working space and restrictions to other engineering activities on-site. These *in situ* remediation technologies include physical methods such as soil vapor extraction and pump-and-treat, chemical methods such as soil flushing and solidification/stabilization, and biological methods such as bioremediation and phytoremediation.

Full Concealment

Full concealment includes the placement of a cap and engineered cover system to seal the contamination in place in the ground. A number of the technologies that are used in full concealment include earthworks structures composed of a clay cap, geotextile layers on top, and clean soil coverage. In certain situations a perimeter slurry wall surrounds the earthworks structure to provide additional protection and support. The advantage of full concealment is the engineered separation of pollutants that would otherwise be expensive to remediate or remove from the site. The disadvantages of full concealment include the continued presence of the contamination on site and the need to ensure that the full-concealment area is not disturbed or penetrated by digging or construction activities at a later time. The most complete example of full concealment is a landfill where capping and new soil cover is used to encapsulate hazardous materials or industrial waste over the entire site.

Nonintrusive Cleanup

The nonintrusive approach uses natural or benign remediation technologies that leave the site in its original condition and uses where possible but ensures that soil and groundwater contamination is remediated. This requires the application of remediation technologies that use either the natural elements of sun, moisture, and wind in natural attenuation and land farming, as well as microbes and living plant materials in phytoremediation or bioremediation to actively break down pollutants in the soil. The advantage of nonintrusive cleanup is that it presents a more benign and sustainable approach to site remediation while addressing the presence of pollutants. The disadvantage is that the presence of certain pollutants can require other, more aggressive, remediation approaches, and many of these remediation technologies are still in the emerging technology phase.

Who Determines How Contaminated It Is?

Site information regarding the location, concentration, and state of pollutants is prepared and analyzed by environmental experts, including environmental engineers, licensed site professionals (LSPs), and licensed environmental professionals (LEPs).

The work of LEPs and LSPs includes the collection of information on potential pollutants from activities such as site history reviews and interviews, screening methods, sampling and analysis, monitoring wells, geophysical techniques, remote sensing techniques, and laboratory analysis. In parts of the country where there are no LEPs and LSPs, this work is carried out by hydrogeologists, environmental engineering companies, or environmental consultants. The evaluation of contamination on the site and the remedies to reduce or remove is generally carried out in the following sequence of five individual phases:

1. Initial site investigation
2. Comprehensive site assessment
3. Identification, evaluation, and selection of comprehensive remedial action alternatives
4. Implementation of selected remedial action alternatives
5. Operation, maintenance, and/or monitoring of comprehensive remedial actions

Phase I: Initial Site Investigation

History reviews and interviews are conducted first by planners, landscape architects, environmental engineers, or licensed site professionals. These include a thorough review of existing site and topography maps, aerial photographs, building plans, engineering drawings, historical surveys, Sanborn Fire Insurance maps, flood insurance documents, leases, and deeds, as well as historic photographs of the site (see Figure 3.3). If possible, interviews may be carried out with present or former employees who worked on the site to determine not only the details of manufacturing processes and site activities, but also to obtain useful information on locations of former industrial processes on-site and the vicinity of industrial waste that was stored or disposed of on-site legally or illegally. Key issues to be covered are as follows:

- street address as well as latitude and longitude of site
- topographic map
- number of workers on site
- residential population within a fixed radius
- uses of surrounding land
- institutions with 500 feet of site
- natural resources with 500 feet of site

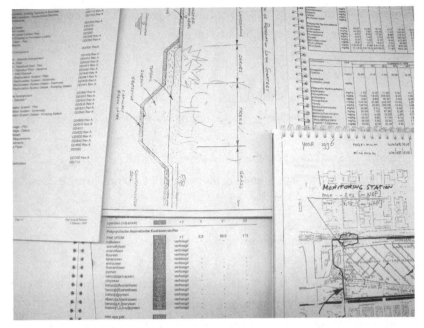

Figure 3.3. A broad array of documents are necessary to conduct the review component of an Environmental Site Assessment for brownfields (photo by Niall Kirkwood).

- site map to scale
- site history
- disposal and releases history
- previous site operations
- oil/hazardous material usage
- waste management
- environmental permits and site compliance
- site hydrogeological characteristics, including soil type (porosity and permeability)
- groundwater flow conditions
- nature and extent of contamination
- migration pathways and exposure potential
- evaluation for immediate "response actions" on-site instigated by regulators to remove site pollutants that pose immediate health problems

The possible outcomes after completion of the Phase I include the following:

- The site meets the regulatory closure requirements without carrying out any further action.
- The site requires further investigation and response to be carried out in further phases.
- The site is identified with "down gradient property status," which would allow the site owner to postpone cleaning up contamination on the property if adequate safety steps are taken, such as erecting a perimeter fence. (The down gradient status refers to the location of the site in relationship to the source of an off-site contamination plume.)

Phase II: Comprehensive Site Assessment

Screening methods carried out by licensed site professionals or environmental engineers correlate data regarding the existence and concentrations of contaminants derived in the laboratory with data obtained on-site. By reducing the quantity of sampling, such methods can be used to guide expensive assessment and remediation projects in the field, thereby minimizing testing, sample preservation and shipment, and analysis expenses. Poor decisions, particularly at remote locations, can result in excessive assessment and remediation costs and can cause unnecessary delays; therefore the use of site-screening technologies should be carefully planned. It is critical to understand the type and quality of data that will be generated before field screening methods are purchased and used in the field. Also, the interpretation of the data generated using field-screening methods should be carefully evaluated before any conclusions are drawn. Key steps to be followed include:

- Analyze all Phase I data in greater detail.
- Decide on the environmental fate and transport (if necessary) of oil or hazardous materials.
- Determine the nature and extent of contamination.

- Update the history of disposal of industrial waste materials on the site.
- Update assessment of hydrogeological characteristics.
- Assess exposure levels.
- Characterize risk.

Screening methods that are employed to determine the level of contamination include the following:

Immunoassays

Immunoassay field screening is designed to measure the presence and concentration of a variety of petroleum hydrocarbon mixtures. Concentration determinations are based upon response to specific types of organic compounds or molecular structures present in all hydrocarbon mixtures. It is possible to monitor for gasoline, diesel, and other hydrocarbon mixtures using immunoassay methods.

Photo-ionization Detectors

The photo-ionization detector (PID) uses ultraviolet light to ionize gas molecules; it is commonly employed in the detection of volatile organic compounds (VOCs).

Soil Gas Surveys

Soil gas is a term describing gas that fills the tiny voids between soil particles. When groundwater is contaminated with VOCs, the chemicals can change into a gas and move upward through the soil and into site areas and buildings. When soil-gas surveys are used during the initial stages of a site investigation, they can rapidly identify VOCs in the subsurface soils.

X-ray Fluorescence (XRF) Techniques

Each element such as lead, zinc, or cadmium found in soils, vegetation, or generally in the environment has a unique set of energy levels. Each element produces a unique x-ray, allowing one to non-destructively identify and measure the elemental composition of a sample, whether it is a leaf or soil. The process of emissions of these characteristic x-rays is called x-ray fluorescence, or XRF, and the associated laboratory analysis is called x-ray fluorescence spectroscopy.

Sampling Analysis

The analysis of contamination in soils, groundwater, and sediments can be carried out either by using localized testing around known polluted areas or by indiscriminately testing locations to gain a broad picture of an entire study area. A more systematic approach uses coordinates or a grid structure superimposed on a map and then transferred to the actual site. The approach to environmental collection varies depending on the complexity and scale of the site area and the objectives of the study. How is the best approach determined? In many ways, it is similar to conventional site sampling to test for soil chemistry, pH, texture, and structure in that it is dependent on the individual nature of the site and the experience of the site operators.

GRAB

"Grab" or individual sampling is specific to a precise location identified on base site maps. These samples, if sufficient in number, can be used to gain a broad picture of the pollutants in soil as well as the subsoil conditions in an entire study area.

COMPOSITE

Composite samples combine individual samples to develop a single characteristic sample of a larger study area. This averages out results and gives a general picture of the pollutants present.

INTEGRATED

Integrated sampling requires the collection of the samples over time in the same location or medium. This allows comparative measurements to be taken, mainly for waterborne contaminants.

Monitoring Wells

The purpose for the installation of vertical monitoring wells located in the soil and subsurface area is to give specific access to the groundwater so that a "representative" view of the subsurface hydrogeology can be obtained. This is done either through the collection of water samples or the measurement of physical or hydraulic parameters. Each monitoring well should be designed and installed to function properly throughout the entire anticipated life of the monitoring program. Several components need to be considered in monitoring well design:

- well diameter
- casing and screen material
- screen length
- depth of placement
- sealing material
- well development

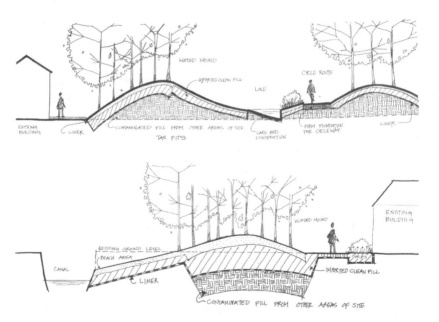

Figure 3.4. Subsurface diagrams (illustrations by Luisa Oliveira).

- well security and maintenance, particularly with locking devices
- length of time required for monitoring
- proper abandonment

Geophysical Techniques

Geophysical technologies locate below-ground features and forms in a nonintrusive way allowing a picture to be built up of subsurface conditions in two or three dimensions. Ground penetrating radar (GPR) operates by transmitting low-powered microwave energy into the ground via an antenna. The GPR signal is reflected back to the antenna by materials with contrasting electrical (dielectric and conductivity) and physical properties. It provides a cross section of objects below the ground such as concealed drums and oil storage tanks that can direct further localized ground-survey methods. See Figure 3.4 for an example of a capping proposal for subsurface contamination using a cross section.

A terrain-conductivity survey measures conductivity without electrodes or direct soil contact. This technique applies electric and magnetic currents to determine the locations of metal objects and conductive bodies, such as underground storage tanks, sludge, and leachate from landfills.

Remote Sensing Techniques

Remote sensing uses electromagnetic radiation that is emitted or reflected to acquire and interpret non-immediate geospatial data from which to extract information about features, objects, and classes of built elements on the land surface. For example, remote sensing uses film photography or infrared techniques to determine the physical extent of ground disturbance, vegetation loss, or surface contamination.

The possible outcomes after completion of the Phase II are the following:

- The site meets closure requirements and no further action is required to take place.

- Comprehensive remedial actions are necessary and the evaluation can proceed to Phase III.

Phase III: Identification, Evaluation, and Selection of Comprehensive Remedial Action Alternatives

The entire team, including the client group, is involved in the following activities coordinated by the planner and the licensed site professional. The key issues to be covered are as follows:

- *Initial screening of alternatives*
  A range of alternative remediation approaches and technologies are assembled in a chart that identifies each technology, the costs associated with each technology, and the length of time required to carry out each remedial activity.
- *Detailed analysis of alternatives that will include bench-scale or pilot testing*
  A more exhaustive spreadsheet and report are developed, outlining the pros and cons of each technology for the reduction or removal of on-site pollutants, including site conditions, performance of technology, and community issues regarding environmental disturbance such as noise, dust, and working hours.
- *Selection of optimum remedial action alternative to implement on-site*
  After review of the initial detailed analysis of alternative remedial alternatives, one approach is selected that supports environmental removal, economic budgetary, and regulatory approvals, as well as community input where appropriate.
- *Preparation of a remedial action plan*
  The environmental engineer or licensed site professional will prepare an action plan for the site (see Figure 3.5 for an example of sampling analysis included in such a plan). The action plan is a document that outlines the protocols and operations on-site for the remedial technology, the technology specifications and outcomes, and the site procedures for personnel, including safety procedures.

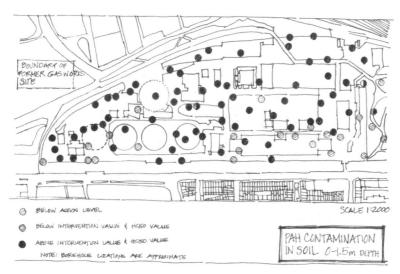

Figure 3.5. An example of Sampling Analysis (illustration by Luisa Oliveira).

The outcome after completion of Phase III is a remedial action plan ready to address the on-site environmental contamination.

Phase IV: Implementation of Selected Remedial Action Alternative

The licensed site professional and the environmental site contractor are mainly involved in this phase; however, the rest of the team, including planners and designers, will be involved in the coordination of remedial actions and technologies with other non-remedial construction activities.

Key issues to be covered are as follows:

- *Documentation of construction*
  Site documents, including plans, layout drawings, and schedules, are prepared to allow bidding and selection of an environmental contractor and the preparation for, and implementation of, the remediation work on site.
- *Implementation of remedial action plan and final inspection*
  The environmental contractor carries out the execution of the action plan on-site according to the details of the construction documentation, to

include all oversight and inspection and signing-off of the work according to the action plan.

The outcome after completion of the Phase IV: the remedial action plan has addressed on-site environmental contamination.

Phase V: Operation, Maintenance, and/or Monitoring of Comprehensive Response Actions

Environmental consultants, licensed site professionals, and often environmental contractors are involved in ongoing operations and maintenance, and they report to federal and state regulatory authorities and through them to the team.

Key issues to be covered are as follows:

- operations and maintenance
- performance monitoring
- "fine tuning" the ongoing long-term remediation, such as pump-and-treat installations

Conclusions

The site stakeholder(s) and all members of the team, including planners and designers, must be familiar with the selected remedial action plan in relation to the existing site conditions and the proposed land-use and design considerations for planning and reuse. These include site opportunities and constraints arising from the demolition or partial removal of site structures such as existing buildings, roads, and infrastructure; the dredging or filling of canals, ponds, and lagoons; the stockpiling of waste material to be removed off-site; and the unavoidable disturbance to plant and wildlife communities. In addition, the removal of natural features such as topsoil, subgrade layers, and vegetation, and the placement of excavations, test pits, monitoring wells, and areas housing on-site remediation equipment all need to be taken into account in the land-use and site-design phases, particularly for equipment that is to remain.

CHAPTER 4

Land Use and Design Considerations

There are several key land-use and design factors to be found in the reuse and redevelopment of brownfields that differentiate them from non-brownfield projects. First, reuse provides an opportunity to reclaim land for use by a private individual, company, or public entity that is currently abandoned, derelict, or underused because of changes in industrial production and/or on-site environmental problems. This includes the restoration and adaptive reuse on-site of former industrial manufacturing and storage buildings as well as engineered structures such as landfills, canals, holding ponds, and roadways. Brownfields are often portrayed as places ravaged by harsh industrial processes and use over time, which reflects an anxiety about the future usefulness of the brownfield site as well as the surrounding land and waterways. The reclamation of brownfield land in developed or developing urban areas is an excellent design opportunity to fill in the urban core and, in urban or exurban areas, to carry out design and planning activities that bring back to life project sites that are visual and environmental eyesores.

Second, the land is elevated to a higher and better use—for example, from heavy industrial to commercial. This is based on the idea that through reuse, the potential of the site itself and its proximity to other urban amenities can be fully realized. Third, the brownfield project can potentially alter the land uses adjacent to and surrounding the project site. Once the land has been changed through design to provide new amenities and programs, and through removing the stigma of an abandoned or underutilized former industrial site, it can immediately start to positively affect the surrounding land, communities, and neighborhoods, especially if it is located in a district where other urban design or redevelopment projects are already in place. These may take the form of urban renewal plans developed by the municipality, or master plans for retail or cultural districts, or Main Street revitalization. These proposals will encourage the cleanup of other abandoned brownfield sites and will facilitate the progress of the larger-scale urban-design projects. This provides design opportunities for further site development of, for example, transportation, infrastructure, open space, and mixed-use projects rebuilding downtown centers, main streets, or former industrial districts. Brownfields can serve a broad range of new uses, including housing, commercial and retail, light industrial, recreation, and open space.

HOUSING

Housing for both the private and public marketplace is an increasingly common new use for former brownfield land (see case study on page 110). The location of brownfield land close to urban centers, transportation links, and often river corridors, lakefronts, and open space make them attractive new land uses that revitalize neighborhoods, provide in many cases much-needed accommodation from affordable housing units to high-end cooperatives and townhouses, and accordingly stimulate other design and construction activities. The adaptive reuse of existing factory or mill buildings for condominium and apartment living has arisen particularly in older manufacturing areas where the building stock on brownfield sites has architectural merit in terms of structural integrity, large floor-to-ceiling heights, and the existing provision of good natural light and ventilation, as well as durable construction materials.

In cases where total demolition of former structures is called for rendering a cleared site, townhouse projects have been proposed establishing new districts and subdivisions of single-family homes, roads, and amenities on former industrial land. But not all former industrial lands are appropriate for residential use. An industrial rail corridor, for example, might not be a suitable place for new housing, but the following new uses might be a better fit (see Figure 4.1).

Figure 4.1. View along semi-abandoned rail corridor looking toward downtown Boston, Massachusetts (photo by Luisa Oliveira).

COMMERCIAL AND RETAIL

Recycling a brownfield site for mixed land uses, such as commercial and retail, becomes possible when a larger brownfield project is broken down into design phases over time. This allows for multiple site programs to be planned for the site. In addition, the nature of brownfield risk-based remediation allows for certain parts of the brownfield site to become available earlier for development than others. Many brownfield sites are located on major thoroughfares, making them suitable for transformation to commercial and retail land uses.

LIGHT INDUSTRIAL

There are instances where a former brownfield site can still maintain its industrial land use but can be altered from an older polluting heavy industry to a cleaner regulated light industry providing research and development laboratories or smaller manufacturing facilities (see case studies on pages 68 and 110). These are often assembled on cleared and remediated brownfield sites or are integrated into adaptive reuse design approaches where new buildings and infrastructure are proposed around existing built forms. The advantage of using former manufacturing sites for new light-industry land uses is that transportation connections are already in place, as well as utilities, including sewerage and power.

RECREATION AND OPEN SPACE

An increasingly important land use arising from brownfields, particularly within the inner city, is the development of recreational, sports, and open space ranging from waterfront promenades on former port lands and harbors, biking greenways and new urban golf courses on closed landfill sites, and all forms of outdoor recreation and sports fields (running tracks, football, soccer, baseball, and tennis). The recreational or open space may be at the scale of a major greenway (see case study on page

80), or at the scale of neighborhood playgrounds and community "pocket parks" on individual local brownfield sites such as former gas station, dry cleaners, and small manufacturing complexes. A recent land-use trend is growing centers and community gardens on derelict land, providing interim or longer-term urban agricultural uses adjacent to residential neighborhoods. Outside or on the edge of the city, larger-scale open-space uses found on former brownfield lands include wetlands restoration, open parkland, and habitat restoration in areas of ecological sensitivity and scientific interest.

INTERIM LAND USES

While brownfield development may take a number of years in total to achieve, temporary land uses can be proposed and initiated on-site in the short term. The designer should be aware of the range of initial uses that can be accommodated on a brownfield, including solar energy generation ("brightfields" programs by the U.S. Department of Energy), biofuel production, interim food and craft markets, recreational facilities, seasonal entertainment, and art venues. Another form of interim land use is the evolving site use, where initial short-term cultural uses, for example, are replaced in time by light industrial or retail, which are replaced after ten years by permanent housing as dictated by economics and the marketplace. This allows vacant brownfield land to have productive uses for the earlier years of a long-term project, rather than standing idle.

A more-recent phenomenon is the identification of brownfield sites for long-term acquisition by a municipality or public planning agency. In some cases, there may be no detailed land-use proposals for a brownfield other than the "bundling" of adjacent or conjoined sites—say, along a railway corridor. This will allow for smaller sites that may have limited land-use potential to form part of a larger network of sites, or for a larger site to maximize its potential.

Other land-use considerations to be taken into account are related to the restrictions imposed by Activity Use Limitations (AULs) on the design and planning activities for a brownfield. (See chapter 2 for a description of the legal, liability, and environmental considerations of AULs.) From a design point of view, AULs impose restrictions on the future use of certain parts of the site where layers of undisturbed contamination lie. A common example of an AUL is the permanent capping by an asphalt surface of a discrete area of soil contamination, usually on the back perimeter of a site to create a parking zone that must remain in perpetuity. The AUL location in this case is clearly determined by previous land uses onsite and by the placement of industrial storage or the former dumping of waste material close to a site boundary. AULs are considered a significant factor in determining the physical planning of brownfield sites, as they limit the designer's flexibility in placing buildings, parking, open space, and new utilities.

WHY IS IT IMPORTANT FOR DESIGNERS TO BE ON BOARD IN A BROWNFIELD PROJECT?

As the economic, social, cultural, ecological, and other potentials of brownfields become recognized, new land uses and programs are proposed, plans for redevelopment are drawn up, and methods are sought to clean up the despoiled sites, returning them once again to productive use. This is both a new and an old activity. It is old because the process of recycling land has been going on since antiquity. It is new because of the relative magnitude and exotic nature of the pollutants involved today, and correspondingly, the interdisciplinary design strategies and creative programs required for rectification and reuse. In addition, it involves a greater number of stakeholders and other interested parties than ever before. This in turn has led to sometimes contentious debate about the future of these sites and has created rifts between those who support development or preservation of land, sustainable community activities or commerce, private or public use.

One of the important roles of the designer in brownfields reuse is to address some of the inherent conflicts and tradeoffs that exist in bringing contaminated land and buildings into new uses. In particular, the de-

signer has to understand the role of remediation as it relates to the design and implementation of the project—for example, the relationship of
sub-grade excavations, the removal of contaminated site material, or the
realignment of strata on the site through placement of contaminated material and capping activities to the physical planning and program development that takes place. In addition, the phasing of remediation technologies that may occur over time requires planning and design activities
to take account of temporary (or not so temporary in some cases) remediation equipment and processes, such as pump-and-treat systems with
supporting buildings and monitoring wells or the placement of on-site
capping techniques. In this the designer has to ensure that the environmental engineering site-work, including testing and site sampling of soil
and groundwater, is coordinated with the master planning activities on
the brownfield.

In particular, the designer has to understand the cut-and-fill balance of
soil on the site, the structural integrity of the ground, the sequence of excavations and moving of material, the protection of mature vegetation to
be saved, and the need to install or upgrade utilities below ground. The
designer has to take a lead in coordinating these activities, as well as the
many other consultants who may be engaged in the project from an economic, regulatory, engineering, transportation, and historic restoration
point of view. This includes all the outreach and community involvement, as well as participation of the diverse stakeholders involved in a
brownfield site. These may include not only adjacent site owners and municipal agencies but also various city groups and nonprofit organizations
that may be engaged in urban-renewal activities, community environmental justice, or redevelopment projects. In these cases the designer par-
ticipates in communicating many aspects of the brownfield project to
these groups as the project develops as well as to neighborhood audiences
at required public meetings.

Of particular importance is the designer's role in producing not only
graphic materials that demonstrate the benefit of the proposed project to
the community but also materials that can help to bridge the comprehen-
sion gap between, on the one hand, complex scientific and engineering

data and survey results, and, on the other hand, the perceived brownfield site conditions. This is accomplished through written and diagrams explaining the various remediation strategies to be employed, their effects, and public-health outcomes to protect the community and the long-term sustainability of the site. The designer is employed here to develop a new story for the site, one that either breaks from the past land uses or employs parts of the previous site buildings, open space, and infrastructure to aid in the regeneration of the site.

Through the design process, the designer on a brownfield project establishes the initial creative vision and the project's identity in terms of the regeneration and recovery of the land from former polluting industrial land uses to a higher and better use (see Figures 4.2a and 4.2b). This initially can take the form of cleaning up existing pollutants in the soil, surface water and groundwater, and structures in order to meet appropriate regulatory standards as planned and overseen by the environmental engineer or licensed site professional.

The design process must also go beyond basic remediation and site planning to include the integration of a broader set of site principles related to sustainable development of the land in order to ensure that no further brownfields are created and to provide further amenities on the site for the surrounding community. Among the activities the designer can undertake is informing the team about the community's vision for the brownfield site. Usually the surrounding residents and neighborhoods did not contribute to the contamination. In addition, the community has typically been limited in their ability to improve their community, whether through new development, job creation, or neighborhood amenities, due to the barriers associated with a contaminated brownfield site. Here the designer's strategy is based on the need to make communities more livable for existing residents and to attract more homes, potential employment, and recreation back into the community. The designer will interact and communicate with the local community through outreach and public meetings. In these meetings the role of the designer can vary, although the designer's main purpose is to clearly communicate the relationship between design proposals for the land and the remediation

Figures 4.2a and 4.2b. Brownfields reuse, before and after (illustration by Luisa Oliveira).

process, and particularly to address the stigma and perception of pollution that may still persist on the site and surroundings. The designer needs to demonstrate that through the redevelopment and regeneration of the site the issue of pollutants will be addressed, and that the reuse and development creates employment, provides amenities, and is sustainable within the neighborhood.

Further, the designer provides vision and leadership by acknowledging that there is no single generic approach to brownfield sites, by recognizing and enhancing the context and qualities of a site, and by using good design and planning principles. In all these ways, the designer sets an example that builds brownfield literacy and capacity to all stakeholders.

WHAT ARE THE LAND USE AND DESIGN CONSIDERATIONS IN A BROWNFIELD PROJECT?

The provision of infrastructure and/or connections to existing transportation, open space systems, and river protection are some of the key considerations when initially reviewing the potential of a brownfield site. Generally, one of the elements that urban brownfield lands have in common is that they have appropriate infrastructure already in place—for example, road and often rail access as well as public transport, power, communications, and sewerage. These amenities make these sites attractive for future development and for private real-estate markets. Infrastructure can also be considered to be extended to include fiber-optic ductways to serve new IT businesses, educational facilities, and residences; new or reworked storm-water systems to capture rainwater before it leaves the site; and the potential planning of connections to adjacent airport hubs and proposed upgraded public transit, bike, and pedestrian pathways.

Land-use considerations regarding the sustainable nature of brownfield development will add additional site programs concerned with integration of the land with public transportation, walking access to the site from transport hubs, the provision of bicycle paths, the compactness of building development, and the restoration of rivers and waterways on-site. Historic preservation of buildings and structures on site and the adaptive reuse of any existing industrial structures is a benefit of brownfield development.

Following remediation that imposes capping on-site to separate potential human and environmental contact with in-ground contamination, land uses may be restricted to only individual buildings and parking. An example is a Head Start day-care facility located on a brownfield in Somerville, Massachusetts, where the in-ground pollutants resulted in an Activity Use Limitation (AUL), and a site-capping strategy was imposed over

the entire site area, removing the opportunity for the provision of outdoor activity spaces for the children. The city acquired another adjacent
small parcel of less polluted brownfield land to remediate and develop a
community garden with raised beds and a children's playground to provide the necessary outdoor space for the Head Start facility. Thus the adjacent land uses changed to accommodate the conditions and proposed
program of the original brownfield site, providing not only more community amenities but removing the stigma of brownfield land development in the neighborhood.

Unlike many conventional developments where building footprints
and open space infrastructure are dispersed on a site according to, for example, economy of space, functional relationships, and ease of access,
brownfield lands require considerations of the existing ground surface,
sub-grade, groundwater, and in many cases the precise location of building structures through the relationship between remediation and site design. Another consideration is the selection of site programs in relationship to remediation over time. For example, where on-site operations to
remove contamination are phased over years, development programs occur in a staggered fashion as portions of land become available. This is
particularly important where vehicular and pedestrian movement and
road and pathway locations are involved in establishing the framework
for site development.

Finally, steps have to be taken by the designer to ensure that a new
brownfield is not created on the site through sustainable practices in site
development and construction, as well as site operations and future management of waste on- and off-site.

SOILS

The provision of both soils to be used as sub-grade and fill material, and
also imported or recycled organic soils for vegetation areas, has to be
carefully considered on a brownfield site. After the completion of any
necessary building demolition, many consultants have turned to soil

excavation and removal as the remedy in addressing contaminated soils at brownfields because of speed and reliability. Once new topographic site levels have been established, the site will typically have a shortfall of sub-grade or fill material. The designer has to balance the importation of new material with the recycling of older non-contaminated soil. Certain ex-situ soil remediation technologies, such as thermal desorption, leave a re-sulting inert material lacking organic matter that can be stockpiled and reused on-site as fill where needed.

STORM WATER AND SITE DRAINAGE

A key element of storm-water management on brownfields is the treat-ment and storage of storm water rather than infiltration into the ground. This requires the designer to develop site approaches that retain, treat, and release storm water over time without coming into contact with the contaminated soils—for example, through green roofs or storm-water gardens. At a brownfield site under design preparation for recycling and reuse, many of the existing impervious surfaces, whether roads, drive-ways, loading docks, or sidewalks, may still remain in place. All these sur-faces, whether they remain or are replaced by newer construction, pre-vent rainwater soaking back into the ground, and they also speed up and increase the quantity of run-off from the site into adjacent swales and rivers.

Capping parts of the site as a remediation strategy creates even more impervious surfaces. The cap acts not only as an engineered layer be-tween the inhabitants of the site and below-ground contamination but also as a waterproof barrier to prevent migration through the soil of wa-ter that may carry additional pollutants into groundwater and off-site. This requires the designer both to plan for a greater impervious surface area on-site, and to address the continuing issues of the remaining imper-vious roadway and hardscape surfaces. This can require the introduction of a "living" infrastructure that combines vegetated and soil areas with the under-drain systems that are required to divert water above the cap for on-site water infiltration and reuse rather than allowing it to drain into the sewer systems.

VEGETATION

Living systems of adaptive and native plants can exist throughout a brownfield site, especially if it has been abandoned for a number of years. Observation of vegetation on an initial site visit can indicate the overall health of the ecological systems of the site and can also indicate potential problem areas. While most of the vegetation is cleared during a site excavation, the following, if found on-site, should be considered of value and should be integrated into future development and reuse proposals: large individual canopy trees, boundary hedgerows of mixed canopy trees and shrubs, clumps or groupings of flowering trees adjacent to open grass areas, and vegetation adjacent to river corridors, ponds, pools, and canals. A full survey of existing vegetation needs to be carried out by a horticulturalist or ecologist in order to determine the value of the existing trees and shrubs in the overall larger pattern of open space and urban vegetation corridors.

The designer has a very significant role related to the land-use and design opportunities afforded by brownfields. Today abandoned industrial sites are often the last available areas in the urban fabric where new projects can be created. The departure of industry and the remaining brownfield lands creates the chance to make a dramatic improvement in the living qualities and environment of the city, and in this respect the creation of high-quality public space is just as important as the construction of new homes or workspaces. City parks created on brownfields can in turn become important places of encounter—not only for dog-walkers, joggers, skaters, cyclists, or Sunday-afternoon soccer players, but for the entire city as places for concerts and other special cultural events.

CHAPTER 5

Case Studies

Through background research and interviews with individuals involved with brownfields, we found that case studies give both experienced and first-time brownfield redevelopers a better understanding of how different techniques, programs, and uses can be applied. Most important, case studies can demonstrate how stakeholders overcome difficulties and show future stakeholders how brownfield cleanup and redevelopment can be completed successfully. After researching brownfield projects all over the country, we chose five case studies that highlight the variety of challenges, lessons, and techniques that are a part of the brownfield experience—with each one being run by a first-time brownfields team. While all of the case studies include related lessons, each presents a different story and experience. That first encounter with the brownfields world was rough for many of the individuals we spoke with, but each of these stories offers key insights about what worked and what did not. For each case study, the formula presented in chapters 2 through 4 is put into action. We show how missing community outreach or choosing a less-than-ideal remediation strategy can hamstring a project, but that attention to a few essential steps can keep a project on track.

The story of the Steel Yard, in Providence, Rhode Island, presents some of the challenges often faced by small nonprofits, such as capacity and management issues, community outreach, and relationship and team building. The story is also about the preservation of the site's unique history and the creative remediation and design solutions employed.

The Assunpink Creek Greenway Project in Trenton, New Jersey, highlights two crucial lessons: (1) how to employ creative problem solving to deal with flooding, and (2) how to stay focused on long-term goals. When faced with a vast stretch of derelict industrial buildings in a floodplain, city leaders, with the support of key federal resources, devised a solution that conserved the land for public use—a bold move that solved both the problem of what to do with abandoned buildings and how to accommodate buildings in a flood plain. With a timeline of multiple decades, this project shows the importance of patience when a commitment has been made to completing a project successfully.

The Delta Sigma Theta project in Portland, Oregon, is a very different example of a nonprofit experience. With no contamination, the project has been able to focus on the design and community factors rather than cleanup. The project is a prime example of an inventive and localized green building project: it demonstrates not only how to achieve the successful conversion of a gas station, but also how to respond successfully to the needs of its community.

The Eastern Fine Paper project in Brewer, Maine, is a rare one, because it has successfully brought industrial jobs back to a brownfield site. Through the organization, networking, and determination of the city of Brewer, they were able to complete the project very quickly. This case study demonstrates how consistent and organized efforts can lead to the renewal of a complex brownfield site in a very short time.

The last case study, the Watershed at Hillsdale project located in Northwest Portland, Oregon, highlights a creative use for an underutilized and challenging piece of land. Throughout the project's development, the surrounding neighborhood and business leaders played a large role in its success. Addressing a number of specific community needs, this project includes affordable senior housing and incorporated a variety of green building techniques.

The chosen cases are not intended to be representative, and they hardly provide a full representation of the possible geographic settings or re-development challenges of brownfields. Our focus is explicitly domestic, so all of the cases we chose are in the United States. Also, the cases do not cover the vast array of unique contamination and redevelopment circumstances which exist. In particular, we have not included any cases in the South and Midwest. But exhaustive geographic coverage is not our aim here; instead, we invite the reader to see how the principles of brownfields regeneration described in the preceding chapters work in a few states and in a few different configurations, even when rich and sophisticated experience is lacking. These are the stories of first-time brownfields regeneration stumbles and successes.

THE STEEL YARD,
PROVIDENCE, RHODE ISLAND

PROJECT BACKGROUND

The Steel Yard is a nonprofit industrial arts organization located on a brownfield site in the Valley district of Providence, Rhode Island.[1] The site of The Steel Yard was once home to the Providence Steel and Iron Company (PS&I). The Valley district was a center for industry, with steel manufacturers, foundries, jewelry companies, and more. Today, many other brownfield sites surround The Steel Yard and are scattered throughout its neighborhood. While some sites have been redeveloped into commercial or residential properties, many remain abandoned. The neighborhoods surrounding The Steel Yard traditionally have been some of the

---

BOX 5.1

The Steel Yard

Location:	Sims Avenue, Providence, Rhode Island
Site size:	3 acres
Owner:	Woonasquatucket Valley Community Build (aka The Steel Yard)
Former use:	steel fabrication facility
Current use:	industrial arts educational center
Contaminant(s):	lead-contaminated soil
Team:	Executive Director—The Steel Yard
	Landscape Designer—Klopher Martin Design Group
	Environmental Engineer—E. A. Engineering, Science, Technology Inc.
	Civil Engineer—Morris Beacon
	Electrical Engineer—Griffith & Vary Inc.
	Contractor—Catalano Construction Inc.
Total cost of project:	approx. $1.2 million
Website:	http://www.thesteelyard.org

BOX 5.2

TIMELINE

1902 Builders Iron Foundry opens Structural and Architectural Department.

1905 Department sold and incorporated as the Providence Steel and Iron Co.

1918 Adjoining land acquired for expansion.
Ornamental Iron works building constructed.

1937 Providence Brewing Co. land purchased for second expansion.

2001 Providence Steel and Iron closes.

2002 Site purchased by Milhaus LLC.
Remediation and preservation begins.

2005 Site placed on National Register of Historic Places.

2007 Majority of the site purchased by The Steel Yard nonprofit.

2008 Long-term remediation begins.

2010 Completion of remediation expected in spring.

---

poorest in Providence; however, this area has attracted artists and new development over the past decade.

Two young entrepreneurs, Nick Bauta, a Rhode Island School of Design graduate, and Clay Rockefeller, a Brown University student, decided to purchase the site of the Providence Steel and Iron Company in 2002 to become the home of their new organization, The Steel Yard. Other artists were living and working in the neighborhood and The Steel Yard's founders saw an opportunity to create a unique resource for the local community. The Steel Yard's mission is focused on celebrating the industrial history of its site, redefining the use of industrial practices for workforce development, and using art as a way to approach community development and urban revitalization (see Figures 5.1 and 5.2).

SITE HISTORY

For almost a century, the site at 27 Sims Avenue in Providence, Rhode Island, was home to the Providence Steel and Iron Company. PS&I was a

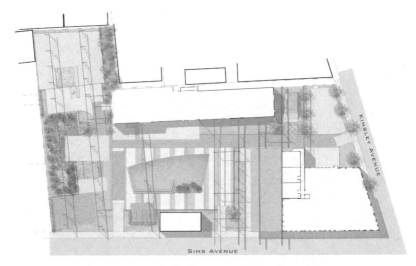

Figure 5.1. Site plan (courtesy of Klopfer Martin Design Group).

Figure 5.2. Area filled with mulch after initial hot-spot removal, 2005 (photo courtesy of David Allyn).

subsidiary of the Builders Iron Foundry, established in Providence in 1822. In 1902 the company built a two-story brick building on 20,000 square feet of land, which would serve as a structural steel shop. Over the next 32 years, PS&I purchased an additional 100,000 square feet of adjacent property. These purchases allowed the company to expand its system of cranes and build an ornamental iron works building and an office building.

Like many other steel manufactures in the United States, PS&I was forced to close its doors early in the 21st century because its operations were no longer financially feasible. However, unlike similar industrial sites in faster-growing cities, PS&I was not torn down to make room for new development. At that time, there was little demand for new development in Providence and the PS&I site was revitalized to serve a new growing population of artists in the neighborhood (see Figure 5.3).

ENVIRONMENTAL CONSIDERATIONS

During the time of operation, PS&I painted its manufactured beams with a spray-on lead-based paint (see Figure 5.4). The painting was done outdoors and the excess paint would drip off the beams onto the soil below. Layers of dried paint could still recently be seen below the areas where the beams were hung. All soils with lead greater than 4,000 ppm were required by the Rhode Island Department of Environmental Management

Figure 5.3. Site being used by The Steel Yard—before final remediation, 2004 (photo courtesy of The Steel Yard).

Figure 5.4. Site during initial phase of cleanup—lead based paint, 2003 (photo courtesy of The Steel Yard).

(RIDEM) to be excavated and treated on-site with a phosphate-based stabilizer. Soils in four areas contained lead at concentrations greater than 10,000 ppm. These soils were removed and disposed of at a licensed facility. Soils with lead between 4,000 ppm and 10,000 ppm were placed back into the site excavations after treatment.

The remediation plans for The Steel Yard include extensive site capping. The capping will include buildings, pavement, two feet of clean soil, and one foot of clean soil with a geo membrane barrier. The construction of the cap will also include pervious pavement and a system of vegetated areas, including rain gardens, bioswales, sites for phytoremediation, and canopy cover. By choice, the capping plan calls for the treatment and re-

Figure 5.5. Site rendering—central space looking north (courtesy of Klopfer Martin Design Group).

tention of the majority of the site's contaminated soils through designed changes in the topography. As part of the capping plan, The Steel Yard will create an 11,800-square-foot green-space amphitheater and lawn (see Figure 5.5). This area will be open to the public and available for markets, community meetings, arts and culture festivals, and environmental education programming. Future development plans include an open-air stage. An additional area of approximately 11,500 square feet of the site's southwest corner will serve as a landscaped sculpture park.

Another component of the site's reuse plan is the Steel Yard Green Fund, an initiative aimed at minimizing the site's environmental impact. Through a comprehensive three-phase strategy, the organization seeks to become a flagship for environmental sustainability with a design that offsets the site's carbon footprint, the greening of its existing industrial processes, and the on-site cultivation of such renewable energy sources as wind, solar, and bio-fuel. It is the goal of the Steel Yard Green Fund to cultivate an energy-self-sufficient industrial facility.

LAND USE AND DESIGN CONSIDERATIONS

To a large extent, the site design was led by the organization's goal to serve as a community organization, public space, and functioning industrial arts center. As explained in chapter 4, designers must consider how their decisions are linked to a community's vision. The Steel Yard has worked with its designers from the Klopher Martin Design Group (KMDG) to do just this. As mentioned above, an amphitheater and raised lawn is being created by using a significant amount of the contaminated soils. Rather than having to remove these soils from the site, KMDG were able to incorporate the capping of the soils into a design that corresponded with the organization's mission and its goals for the site's future uses. This raised area will allow the organization to better accommodate outdoor events such as performances, art fairs, and farmers' markets (see Figure 5.6). In addition to this raised area, other capped sections of the site will be able to serve as outdoor work areas, sculpture gardens, and public space.

In addition to the community considerations, The Steel Yard focused much of their land use and designs around their capping and stormwater plans. The Steel Yard chose to retain much of its contamination on-site— a critical factor in the site design. The organization felt that it was their responsibility to deal with the soil, rather than shipping it elsewhere. While it was also less expensive to do this, there are complications that have surfaced because of this decision. Having to manage all of the contamination on-site, there are a number of areas that can no longer be used for future development on the property. Drake Patten, the Executive Director

Figure 5.6. Site rendering—outdoor amphitheater (courtesy of Klopfer Martin Design Group).

and Project Manager, estimates that about 25 percent of the site will be unusable because of the remediation techniques they have chosen. Other remediation choices, such as transporting the contaminated soils off-site, may have allowed the organization to maximize the site's development potential. This is especially worrisome for the organization, as the economy has changed since the project began and additional uses for the property need to be considered.

Storm-water planning has also played a major role in the design process for The Steel Yard. Working closely with the Narragansett Bay Commission (NBC), The Steel Yard needed to come up with a plan that both satisfied NBC's goal of keeping the site's runoff out of the sewer system, which was consistent with their own goal of using the natural environment to manage their storm water. As mentioned above, The Steel Yard worked with its designers to come up with a system of permeable surfaces, rain gardens, bioswales, and phytoremediation sites that would be able to handle most storms before the runoff would reach the sewer system or the adjacent river. The Steel Yard is still working to refine this system, but they have found their design to be successful so far.

ECONOMICS

Initially, the site of PS&I was purchased by The Steel Yard's founders, Clay Rockefeller and Nick Bauta, and leased by The Steel Yard. However, in 2007 the nonprofit was able to purchase the site. As the owner of the property, The Steel Yard was able to take advantage of a number of funding opportunities that would not have been available to them without their nonprofit status. The organization received $400,000 from the EPA brownfield cleanup grants. In addition, they secured $199,000 from the Rhode Island Economic Development Corporation–managed EPA grant funds and $100,000 from their Revolving Loan Program. These funds have been matched by $300,000 in cleanup work completed by the previous owners (Clay Rockefeller and Nick Bauta) and $100,000 for design-related costs coming from The Steel Yard's private fundraising.

Not only did The Steel Yard benefit from their nonprofit status in regard to grants, but they also were able to receive a variety of in-kind contributions that helped them to bring down their costs. Working closely with their contractor, The Steel Yard found a variety of in-kind construction material contributions. The organization also will be receiving trees on Arbor Day from the Providence initiative Trees 2020, and they hope to find other in-kind donations as they complete the site.

COMMUNITY

The Steel Yard plans for their site to be viewed as a community resource, one where the residents from the surrounding neighborhoods will feel welcome. To ensure that the community was aware of the site cleanup, The Steel Yard planned for an outreach program. In 2007 the organization initiated a two-month plan that included a public meeting and two open-house days at the site. As part of this outreach, the organization placed information about the project in the local library and the newspaper, and they distributed fliers. These documents were in both English and Spanish, and The Steel Yard arranged for a Spanish interpreter for the public meeting. The businesses in the neighborhood were also invited. Unfortunately, these events were unattended.

As The Steel Yard continues to build their site into a unique community resource, they will need to find alternative and creative ways to engage the surrounding residents and businesses. In a community where many families are living below the poverty level, it can be difficult to reach neighbors through typical community advertising methods. The Steel Yard will need to plan for new strategies and find other ways to access the local residents and business owners. The services and programs offered by the organization are valuable, but they will only reach their highest potential when the neighborhood is an active participant.

CURRENT STATUS

The Steel Yard is currently undergoing the final phase of remediation, with the site cleanup to be completed by the spring of 2010. As the organization continues to raise funding they will move forward with the site renovations and landscaping. During this stage the organization has continued their programming, which includes such offerings as industrial

Figure 5.7. Site rendering—pedestrian entry at Sims Avenue (courtesy of Klopfer Martin Design Group).

arts courses, youth programs and partnerships, public art events, and an urban furniture line. The courses for adults include metalworking, ceramics, glass, and jewelry. Working with schools in Providence, The Steel Yard offers many of these courses to youths, as well as mentorship opportunities. Through its urban furniture line, The Steel Yard commissions local artists to produce handmade and one-of-a-kind garbage cans, bike racks, planters, and tree guards. These items can be seen in many communities throughout the state. After operating for the past seven years, The Steel Yard has created a unique space and resource for its community and the state of Rhode Island (see Figure 5.7).

LESSONS LEARNED

The process of remediation has been very difficult for The Steel Yard. As a small organization with only five full-time staff members, they have found it challenging to manage their daily responsibilities and oversee the cleanup of the site. While discussing the site redevelopment, the director, Drake Patten explained, "At times, I wish we had hired a project manager. I've ended up spending 60 to 80 percent of my time on this remediation when I was also running the organization."[2] Having never been involved in a brownfield redevelopment, the organization found the overall process quite difficult to navigate.

The project has spanned three years, and over that time the project team has changed drastically. Like many other projects working with a number of different companies and individuals, The Steel Yard was faced with a great deal of turnover throughout the process. Their initial design firm closed, but fortunately the designer they had been working with opened his own firm and continued the project. In addition, the organization had to work with a variety of environmental engineers, as the original company they hired was bought out and then new people were assigned to the project. The environmental engineers played a crucial role in the project, and having to work with four different people over the three years made it very difficult for the organization to have consistency or to accomplish the necessary tasks to move forward with their permitting in a timely manner.

The biggest challenge for the organization has been working with the Rhode Island state agencies and the variety of departments that were involved with the permitting and approval process for the project. Patten expressed her frustration, explaining that the Rhode Island brownfields program was "totally challenging to work with." The project required substantial involvement of the Rhode Island Department of Environmental Management (DEM), the Rhode Island Coastal Resources Management Council, and the Narragansett Bay Commission. These organizations, and even offices within DEM, seemed unable to work together and cooperate so that The Steel Yard could accomplish their project smoothly. While the continual disruption of the project team may have played a role in some of these complications, it seems that The Steel Yard's experience was one of unnecessary hurdles.

Although The Steel Yard has faced a number of challenges throughout their project, they have also found the experience to be extremely educational and rewarding. Halfway into the remediation, Patten said she wished she had not been the project manager. However, a year later she was able to look at her role very differently. She explained that by being the project manager, she was able to build a very strong relationship with the contractor and other team members, something that a hired manager would probably not have been able to achieve. She also found that her ongoing presence allowed for some additional oversight. If she had not been there every day, some problems might not have been caught until it was too late. In addition to the importance of her own role to the project, she found that her staff was able to connect with the team in a unique way. The staff had a keen interest in the remediation and redevelopment, and the project team was also interested in The Steel Yard's programming. Through their shared experiences and relationships, these groups helped one another reach a point of strong personal commitment and passion for the project and the organization.

ASSUNPINK GREENWAY, TRENTON, NEW JERSEY

PROJECT BACKGROUND

The Assunpink Creek Greenway project in Trenton, New Jersey, when fully completed, will be composed of over 99 acres of urban parks, trails, and reclaimed wetlands along the Assunpink Creek. Leah Yasenchak, an experienced brownfields consultant and former U.S. EPA employee, works as the project manager, overseeing the initiative with the support of a cross section of state regulators, city officials, local citizens, and property owners. From the project's inception in 1999, Yasenchak and her colleagues in the city of Trenton's Department of Housing and Economic Development have pushed forward a vision for the creek as a broader framework for addressing the environmental, health, and related redevelopment issues associated with the brownfield properties that are included in the project area. Under the New Jersey Department of Environmental Protection Brownfield Development Area (BDA) initiative, the project in-

---

BOX 5.3
Assunpink Greenway

Location:	Trenton, New Jersey
Site size:	99 acres (15 brownfield sites)
Owner:	City of Trenton
Former use:	Multiple industrial uses
Proposed use:	Recreational greenway
Contaminant(s):	Variety, including PCBs, PAH, petroleum, metals
Team:	Project manager—Brownfield Redevelopment Solutions
	Landscape architect—consultant
	Parks and Recreation staff—City of Trenton
	Planning staff—City of Trenton
Total cost of project:	Anticipated at over $27 million
Website:	http://www.trentonnj.org/

BOX 5.4

TIMELINE

1906	Fredrick Law Olmsted Jr. plans a greenway in Trenton.
1985	City of Trenton acquires Crescent Wire property.
1995	City begins considering redevelopment strategy for Assunpink Creek area.
1997	Green Acres / Mercer County grant awarded to the city of Trenton to begin acquiring properties.
1997–Present	Acquisition of Properties.
1999	Hurricane Floyd devastates many areas in Trenton when Assunpink Creek floods.
	Project expanded to include other flood-prone properties.
	City receives loan executive from EPA to serve as project manager.
1999	Assunpink Creek Greenway Steering Committee established.
	Planning for Greenway continues.
	Environmental investigation begins.
2000	USEDA funding acquired.
	Second Green Acres / Mercer County grant awarded.
2001–Present	EPA and HDSRF funding used for site investigation and remediation.
2004	City begins acquiring many of the properties.
2005	Brownfield Development Area (BDA) designation.
2007	East Trenton Collaborative established.
2008	City receives Green Acres development funding.
2009–Present	Property acquisitions and cleanups continue.
	Demolition of structures.
?	Estimated date of completion.

---

corporates fifteen different brownfield properties along Assunpink Creek. Once used for a multitude of industrial purposes, all of these properties are now vacant or abandoned. The area's economic depression and high susceptibility to flooding has influenced the city of Trenton to take action

Figure 5.8. Site Plan (courtesy of SPG3).

in the Assunpink Creek area. It is unlikely that these properties will attract private funding for remediation or development, so this approach of public use has given the city the means for renewal (see Figure 5.8).

The city's plan for renewal along the Assunpink Creek includes the establishment of a large linear greenway, which will provide both passive and active recreational amenities in an area that is underserved by such facilities. The conceptual redevelopment plan includes groves of trees, reclaimed wetlands, public art, urban furniture, ball fields, a pavilion, a skate park, and other activity spaces. Not only will the project increase transportation options for the community, including bike paths and access to the train station, but it will also increase educational opportunities and access to a number of historical sites. Through Trenton's brownfields redevelopment efforts, historic resources will be highlighted, including a blacksmith shop that has been in operation since the 1800s, a historical mansion, and an African American cemetery dating back to the 1700s.

While the amenities listed above are vital for the community, the cleanup and redevelopment of the area will also help to mitigate issues of flooding and pollution in Assunpink Creek. Once these sites were acquired as parkland, they were entered into the city's Recreation and Open Space Inventory (ROSI). Inclusion on the ROSI ensures that this green space will be protected and preserved in perpetuity. The project is also a part of the city's larger Open Space Plan, which envisions the redevelopment of brownfields into open space, providing transportation alternatives, flood-damage protection, improved quality of life, improved water quality, and recreational options for a poor minority neighborhood. As the project continues, the city hopes to see an increase in both property values and economic investment in the neighborhoods surrounding the greenway.

SITE HISTORY

Using the Assunpink Creek shoreline as a greenway is not a new idea. According to Yasenchak, in 1906 Fredrick Law Olmsted Jr. planned a similar park for Trenton, but unfortunately the plan was not implemented. After his plan was presented, industry in the area began to steadily encroach on the creek. Contamination and flooding worsened and soon the community's access to the creek was extremely limited. After years of industry and manufacturing, the Assunpink area has become a contaminated and dilapidated area in the community.

In the early 1980s, industry began declining in the area for economic reasons. At this time the city acquired the first property that is part of the greenway project—the Crescent Wire site (see Figure 5.9). In 1997 a small

Figure 5.9. Crescent Wire site before development (photo courtesy of Leah Yasenchak, Brownfields Redevelopment Solutions, Inc.).

Figure 5.10. Crescent Wire site during development (photo courtesy of Leah Yasen-chak, Brownfields Redevelopment Solutions, Inc.).

Green Acres grant was awarded to the city from the state of New Jersey and Mercer County to begin acquiring land for open space. However, it was not until 1999, after a major hurricane devastated the floodplain, that the city began to actively plan for a greenway redevelopment. Although complicated by the ownership status of the properties along the creek, acquisitions were made through a number of different methods. Some sites were taken by eminent domain, while others were foreclosed or purchased from the owner. Property acquisition has been occurring slowly, with over a dozen parcels still in industrial use.

Shortly after the hurricane, Yasenchak arrived in Trenton on loan from EPA. She helped set up a steering committee and the project began to progress.

ENVIRONMENTAL CONSIDERATIONS

The area around Assunpink Creek presents environmental issues on a number of levels. Due to upstream and local construction, the flow of the creek has greatly increased. With few areas for infiltration, storm water simply flows into the creek, bringing with it debris and contaminants from the sites along the shore. During larger rainstorms, the Assunpink can become a powerful stream, putting businesses and homes at risk. Over the years, flooding has caused tremendous financial, emotional, and health damages. In addition to the flooding, the contaminants in the area pose a serious threat to both the ecological balance in the watershed, as well as the health and well-being of the surrounding neighborhoods' residents.

While the greenway is littered with a wide range of former industrial properties, each with its own history of contamination and pollution, the single common denominator among all the parcels is that they all sit on historic fill with high levels of metals and polycyclic aromatic hydrocarbons (PAHs). Throughout the greenway project, and from its very inception, the city of Trenton has invested in characterizing this contamination and remediating it (see Figure 5.11).

The Assunpink Creek Greenway project is a sustainable strategy for addressing contamination, abandoned property, and flooding problems.

Figure 5.11. Enterprise Avenue site before development (photo courtesy of Leah Yasenchak, Brownfields Redevelopment Solutions, Inc.).

Figure 5.12. Enterprise Avenue site after development (photo courtesy of Leah Yasenchak, Brownfields Redevelopment Solutions, Inc.).

By creating almost 100 acres of green space, the project will restore the natural floodplain and replace much of the impermeable surface surrounding the creek in Trenton with permeable grass and other vegetation (see Figure 5.12). Infiltration will be significantly increased and the runoff burden to the creek will be reduced. Site cleanup and remediation will eliminate the exposure to harmful contaminants and decrease the amount of debris and pollution entering the creek.

LAND-USE AND DESIGN CONSIDERATIONS

Under Yasenchak's leadership, the project team includes staff from the city's Planning division, the city's Brownfields Coordinator, a consultant landscape architect, and parks and recreation staff at the city. While highly trained engineers have been used on individual properties, the team itself has strong enough environmental and geological skills and expertise to run the project. The team has worked, off and on, with a steering committee composed primarily of regulatory officials and political and community leaders.

The planners and designers who have been working on the Assunpink Greenway are not pursuing an explicit economic development objective, in contrast to most other brownfield projects. Rather, the project has two primary goals: creation of public green space and storm-water management. Because of these two goals, the land-use and design considerations for the project are very narrowly targeted. The design for each site's remediation is directly affected by the need for increased infiltration. Whereas other brownfields may be able to redirect storm water, the Assunpink Creek cannot handle the current levels of runoff. Therefore, as decisions are made for each site's remediation, the contaminants will need to be dealt with in a way that will both allow for increased infiltration and a significant decrease in contamination in the watershed. Fortunately, the second goal of the project is consistent with the needs of storm-water management. As the designers create public green space and passive recreation areas, they can ensure that landscaping, paths, and paving correspond to the storm-water management plans.

ECONOMICS

The funding and support for the Assunpink Creek Greenway project has come from a number of different sources, including the U.S. Army Corps of Engineers, U.S. Economic Development Administration, EPA, Federal Emergency Management Agency, New Jersey Department of Environmental Protection, New Jersey Economic Development Administration, New Jersey Institute of Technology, Mercer County, engineering and planning firms, planning authorities, and community groups such as the East Trenton Collaborative. Specific funding sources include the NJDEP Green Acres program and the Hazardous Discharge Site Remediation Fund, EPA assessment and clean-up grants, Mercer County Open Space funds, and disaster funding from the USEDA. This outpouring of financial and programmatic support indicates the strong public and institutional sentiment in favor of brownfields reuse in New Jersey.

The project has received some of this funding because of its experience with flooding and the timing of Hurricane Floyd (in 1999). While some unique funding opportunities have helped to make this project possible, they have also complicated it. Being an open-space project with no commercial investment potential (an indirect economic effect of the project is the positive value of a future park to surrounding property owners), the project has had to rely completely on grants and direct city expenditures. In the current economic market, the project has had to put property acquisitions on hold because of funding delays. These constraints have made it difficult to keep up the momentum of the project. However, at the same time, these unique funding sources have allowed the project to exist in the first place. Without funding for open space, it would be impossible for the city to finance the project.

COMMUNITY

Throughout the many stages of this project, it has been difficult to involve and engage the community. During the conceptual phase of the project, three public meetings were held to ask residents what they wanted to see happen and what their needs were. Despite advertising efforts, these meeting were poorly attended. Once the project entered the design phase, the architects and engineers met with small groups of residents to talk to them about their preferences and hopes for the project. However, the scale and extended timeline of the project has made it difficult to keep the community involved and informed. Because the schedule has been unpredictable, it has been impossible to make any promises or give concrete answers to the community. For years it had been difficult to keep the community engaged and excited about the project and at the same time help ordinary residents understand why it was taking so long to complete. It has been a complicated juggling act for the city to keep the community informed.

Fortunately, a positive solution emerged. Local nonprofit organizations joined together to form a group called the East Trenton Collaborative. The primary focus of the group is to revitalize the neighborhood surrounding the greenway project. They have come to serve as the community's primary source of information about the project. This group has been a critical component of the project and through their efforts the community has been galvanized to support the revitalization. The city has found the collaborative to be successful in informing and engaging the community in a way that was impossible for them to achieve working in a top-down fashion. When the East Trenton Collaborative organizes public meetings, they attract over 100 attendees and the meetings tend to advance meaningful dialogue between project team members and community members. This new nonprofit, community-based force on the project offers consistency for the project, in contrast with the relatively frequent shifts in the political winds that pass through City Hall.

CURRENT STATUS

It is hard to imagine that a city could be so committed to a project's success, but Trenton is fully dedicated to completing the Assunpink Creek Greenway project. For over ten years they have been working to move all the phases of the project forward as the plans continue to evolve and grow. With multiple phases in the plans, there is still a very long road ahead of them. As Yasenchak explained, "It has taken us millions of little steps to get where we are today and it will take millions more to complete the project."[3] With every step the city is getting closer to making their goal a reality. This ambitious project may not be completed for a number of years, but it serves as an inspiring example of one city's extreme determination and persistence to better the health and well-being of their community and the environment.

Over the past ten years, the planning process has accelerated and real changes are being seen in the Assunpink Creek area. With continued acquisition, investigation, remediation, demolition, and design, the city is moving along to create an extremely valuable community resource.

LESSONS LEARNED

The most important lessons learned during this project have had to do with patience, determination, and time. Because of the scale of this project and the dependence on so many different stakeholders and funding sources, it has been crucial for the city to recognize that the project is going to take a very long time to complete and the only way to succeed is to move forward with a positive outlook. It would have been very easy for the city to get frustrated and give up. For example, it has taken them more than ten years of on-and-off negotiations to try to acquire just one of the fifteen properties included in the project, and they still have not yet come to an agreement.

However, there is an end in sight. They have learned that it can be challenging in a project of this size to accurately estimate the needed time and money. Permitting can be very complicated and because of funding limitations it had to be done in stages. Acquiring numerous properties is also extremely time-consuming and costly. All due diligence must be completed for each site and additional expenses always arise. Without flexibility and persistence, this project would not be possible.

JUNE KEY COMMUNITY CENTER DEMONSTRATION PROJECT, PORTLAND, OREGON

PROJECT BACKGROUND

The Portland (Oregon) Alumnae Chapter of Delta Sigma Theta Sorority Inc. (an inter-university sorority) has been dedicated to the redevelopment of a brownfield site containing an abandoned gas station in North Portland for more than fifteen years. The group was established in 1945 and is made up of African American college-educated women committed to public service. What has served as a simple meeting space for the group, the brownfield site, is now being transformed into an environmental showcase community center. When completed, the project will provide a space for

---

BOX 5.5

June Key Community Center Demonstration Project

Location:	North Albina Street, Portland, Oregon
Site size:	0.34 acres
Owner:	Portland Alumnae Chapter Delta Sigma Theta Sorority Inc.
Former use:	Gas station / convenience store
Current/proposed use:	Community center / green building demonstration project
Contaminant(s):	none found
Team:	Project Managers—Portland Delta Chapter
	Architect—Nye Architecture
	Construction Consultant—Neil Kelly Design/Build Remodeling
	Other consultants—Fund Development Planning, Real Estate Development, Recycling, Accounting
Total Cost of Project:	approximately $900,000
Website:	http://www.key-delta-living-building.com

BOX 5.6

TIMELINE

1963 Gas station built.

Site used for a number of purposes after gas station closed.

1990 Brownfield report cites that "conditions at site do not appear to pose environmental threat."

1991 Delta Sigma Theta purchases site.

1993 Delta Sigma Theta begins using building as a meeting space.

1997 Site construction options explored.

2003 Graduate students at University of Oregon submit five "green designs."

Design by Toni Garza selected.

2006 Permitting process begins.

2007 Multiple grants awarded.

Sienna Architecture hired for site design.

2008 Environmental assessment completed; no contamination found.

2009 Nye Architecture hired to oversee project design.

2010 Expected completion of Phase 1.

---

daytime programming for seniors, after-school activities for students, and multipurpose uses for the public. Using 50–70 percent recycled resources and sustainability strategies, this green project will serve as a demonstration for other small-to-medium-sized community building projects.[4] The goal of the project is to provide a safe and nurturing environment for children and senior citizens who might otherwise not have a place to gather for academic, intellectual, and social development.

A second phase of the project will include additional meeting spaces and transitional alternative housing to serve a vulnerable population in the community. A current subject of discussion is that this housing will be used for young mothers and their children facing issues such as drug abuse or domestic violence. The timeline for this phase of the project is not yet determined, but the buildings will be made of similar sustainable materials as those used in Phase 1.

SITE HISTORY

In 1963 the gas station on North Albina Street was built. It is unclear when the gas station and convenience store closed, but over the years the site was used for a number of other purposes. In 1991 the Portland Alumnae Chapter of Delta Sigma Theta Sorority Inc. purchased the site, which at that time was abandoned. With the help of family and friends they created a functional gathering space (see Figure 5.13). Although faced with the challenge of the site being a brownfield, over the years the members of the group recognized the site's potential and were assured that it was not actually contaminated. (While hard for some to believe, gas stations can be operated without contaminating land and subsurface water.)

In 1997 the group began exploring the options for construction on the site. They wanted to expand the building into the adjacent vacant lot (also having no known or suspected contamination) and create a safe and nurturing environment that would provide a low- or no-cost meeting space for neighborhood and community organizations, support physical- and mental-health needs in the community, and provide economic-development resources. With leadership from the project manager (one of the members of Delta Sigma Theta) and the support of many local and state

Figure 5.13. Gas station before redevelopment (photo courtesy of Nye Architecture LLC).

agencies, the group has worked diligently to see the project through. The renovated building is expected to open sometime in 2010.

ENVIRONMENTAL CONSIDERATIONS

In 1990 an environmental assessment was done on the gas station site. The assessment found no environmental threats however, because of the time lapse before redevelopment, another assessment was completed in 2008. Again the results came back with no known contamination. Nevertheless, the station was an eyesore and it contributed to blight in the neighborhood. The members of Delta Sigma Theta saw the redevelopment of their meeting center as an opportunity to create a "living building" that would serve as an educational tool and example to others. As mentioned above, the planned community center will use 50–70 percent recycled materials. In addition to using salvaged and recycled materials such as glass and wood obtained from companies and businesses, the building will incorporate surplus metal cargo shipping containers into its structure. The Portland Office of Sustainable Development explains, "Once products are shipped across the ocean, the steel containers that keep materials safe are usually left behind at the port to be recycled or reused for other applications."[5] The sorority and Nye Architecture see the shipping containers as an international salvage source that can be used for many purposes (see Figure 5.14).

Figure 5.14. Site rendering—view from northeast (courtesy of Nye Architecture LLC).

In addition to using sustainable materials, the expanded building will include a large flexible meeting space, increased natural lighting, environmentally innovative heating and cooling, and a water-recycling system. The landscaping will be designed with permeable paving and sustainable native plants. A garden space will be incorporated into the site for the use of a senior citizen and youth garden project.

LAND USE AND DESIGN CONSIDERATIONS

The project is led by Chris Poole-Jones of the Delta Chapter, but she works in close contact with a robust team of planners and designers. Her architect and construction consultant have given the Chapter the necessary technical and design knowledge to make the project happen. The team designed a community outreach strategy that relied primarily on informal networks within the Delta Chapter and a series of focus groups in the neighborhood. The architects worked with Ms. Poole-Jones to run a series of focus groups with Delta Chapter members, which explored how the project could support neighborhood needs.

The result of those focus groups was an emphasis of the team on a primary design goal of the project to support environmental education for the neighborhood. Without the burden of measurable contamination, the group has been able to focus their design around reuse and sustainability. The design focus has therefore been centered on the actual structure of the gas station (the only structure there) and the surrounding lot. The building will be renovated to include a variety of recycled materials, solar panels, and other innovative components. Storm water will be incorporated into a gray-water system and infiltrated using permeable asphalt and bioswales in the surrounding lot (see Figure 5.15). Most important, each of these components will be carefully constructed so that the public can see and learn from them. Education and community involvement are the driving forces behind their design.

ECONOMICS

The funding for the community center has come from a variety of sources. While Delta Sigma Theta has received grants from local, state,

Figure 5.15. Site rendering--view from northwest (courtesy of Nye Architecture LLC).

and federal agencies, they have also taken fundraising to the street. The group has held various events such as garage sales to raise money for the project, but also to educate the community about their plans. Resources have been given to the project from local foundations, corporations (primarily through *pro bono* assistance on technical matters), other nonprofits, and government programs (the City of Portland provided $10,000 and the U.S. EPA provided $25,000, both for environmental testing and investigation). Many of these grants are specifically for green projects. Delta Sigma Theta is fortunate that there is a great deal of financial support in Portland for green design and brownfield projects.

COMMUNITY

The local community has been very involved with the group and the planning for the future community center, particularly through the focus groups run by Delta Chapter members. The president of Delta Sigma Theta explained how they have received nothing but generous support for the project. Other organizations have collaborated on the project, and local residents have supported Delta Sigma Theta at a variety of events. Once the project is completed, the involvement of the community will be the focal point of the demonstration project.

CURRENT STATUS

The neighborhood where the gas station site is located is a well-established residential area. Unlike other neighborhoods in Portland where green buildings are more common, this community is less familiar with brownfield redevelopments, sustainable projects, or using recycled materials in their homes or businesses. By redeveloping this brownfield and constructing a green building in the neighborhood, Delta Sigma Theta hopes to educate and engage the community. Mark Nye, the project's lead architect, says, "There's something very special about this project. It has a great story, and we're leading a new kind of sustainability."[6] Using the community center as a demonstration project, Delta Sigma Theta hopes that they will be able to encourage other small-scale brownfield redevelopments, as well as support their community in using sustainable materials and becoming more conscious of environmental issues in their daily lives.

LESSONS LEARNED

The community center project has been in the planning and preparation stages for over ten years. The group has learned a lot by going through the process, and it has been crucial for them to remain organized and motivated. They have realized how easy it is to forget things, like renewing their permits, when they have been busy working on so many other components of the project. Never having done a green building project, the group has been grateful for all the support and advice given to them from their contractor and architect. Now, however, after going through a large portion of the work, they recognize that it would have been helpful to have more than one person from Delta Sigma Theta managing the project. Volunteering her time, the project manager has found it difficult to do so much on her own. Certain aspects of the project, such as grant writing, were extremely time consuming. It can be easy to overlook how difficult the management will be when a project begins. As Chris Poole-Jones, the project manager, explained, "Only when you are immersed do you realize how complicated it can be."[7]

EASTERN MANUFACTURING FACILITY, BREWER, MAINE

PROJECT BACKGROUND

In 2008 the Cianbro Corporation opened a new facility in Brewer, Maine, on the brownfield site which had previously been occupied by the Eastern Fine Paper Company. The Cianbro Corporation specializes in heavy industrial, energy systems, marine, commercial, and industrial construction. The new modular construction facility builds refinery modules—self-standing building skeletons filled with pipe—and ships the structures by sea to the Gulf of Mexico. Over a period of ten months, the Cianbro Company and the South Brewer Redevelopment, LLC (SBR), transformed the abandoned mill site into a thriving work environment with over 500 jobs (see Figure 5.16). The speed with which this project was

---

BOX 5.7

Eastern Manufacturing Facility

Location:	Main Street, Brewer, Maine
Site size:	41 acres
Owner:	Cianbro Corporation
Former use:	Pulp and paper manufacturing
Current use:	Modular construction facility
Contaminant(s):	Heavy metals, semi-volatile organic compounds, and PCBs
Team:	Site location staff—Cianbro
	Environmental engineers—CES Inc.
	Development staff—City of Brewer
	City planning staff—City of Brewer
Total cost of project:	$16,552,674
Website:	http://www.brewerme.org/Cianbro/modular _site.htm

BOX 5.8

TIMELINE

1889 Eastern Fine Paper opens.

2004 Eastern Fine Paper closes.

2004 Maine DEP conducts initial environmental site assessment and emergency removal activities.

2004 South Brewer Redevelopment, LLC (SBR), obtains ownership of the site.

2005 SBR receives EPA Brownfields Assessment Grant.

2006 SBR receives Brownfields Cleanup Grant.

2007 Cleanup and redevelopment of site begins.

2007 Cianbro receives loan from the EPA Brownfields Revolving Loan Fund.

2008 SBR receives two additional cleanup grants from the EPA.

2008 Cianbro facility completed. Site renamed Eastern Manufacturing Facility.

---

completed contributed greatly to its success. Cianbro called for the redevelopment to be completed—including design, permitting, remediation, and construction—within 12 months. This required a highly coordinated effort between all involved parties. The project team consisted of key Cianbro executives working closely with Brewer city officials and a cadre of environmental engineering consultants.

Not only has the community been thrilled with the outcome, but now Brewer serves as a prime example of workforce development and industrial revitalization for the region. Many cities and towns in Maine face similar issues of disinvestment, but Brewer's story is one of hope and possibility.

SITE HISTORY

The city of Brewer is located in northwestern Maine along the Penobscot River. The city has a rich history in paper manufacturing, and for more

Figure 5.16. Cianbro site after remediation and redevelopment, 2008 (photo courtesy of the Cianbro Corporation).

than 100 years the industry played a large role in the community. In 1889 the Eastern Fine Paper Company began operating a lumber mill, which eventually became a pulp- and paper-manufacturing facility. For ninety years the company was the city's largest employer; at its peak it had over 900 employees (see Figure 5.17). It was also the city's largest taxpayer and sewer user, accounting for one half of the wastewater treatment facility's annual revenues. However, in January 2004 the company filed for bankruptcy and closed the facility, leaving 430 Brewer residents unemployed.

Soon after the closure of the company, the city formed the South Brewer Redevelopment, LLC, to spearhead the redevelopment of the 41-acre property. In May 2004 SBR was able to purchase the site through foreclosure, and in four short years the blighted and contaminated site was transformed into a valuable economic resource for the community. With the help of Maine's Department of Environmental Protection and the federal EPA, the site went through initial environmental assessment and emergency removal activities. By 2007 the final assessment reports were completed and cleanup continued.

Figure 5.17. Eastern Fine Paper Mill, Brewer, Maine, 2005 (photo courtesy of the City of Brewer).

At the start of the cleanup, SBR began looking for opportunities to reuse the property. The Cianbro Corporation approached the group while an adaptive reuse plan was being considered. Because of the site's proximity to deep water and the city's skilled workforce, Brewer was a good fit for Cianbro. In only a year and a half, the cleanup had been completed and the company was open for business. Honoring the site's former occupant, the property was renamed the Eastern Manufacturing Facility.

ENVIRONMENTAL CONSIDERATIONS

Soon after the closure of the Eastern Fine Paper Company, the Maine Department of Environmental Protection initiated an environmental assessment of the site. Results from this assessment indicated that emergency removal of contaminants from the site would be necessary. Specifically, the assessment found drums filled with potentially hazardous materials, metals, and PAHs that exceeded state levels, as well as leaking underground storage tanks. The Maine DEP and EPA Region 1 quickly removed hundreds of drums, totes, and chemical containers. In addition, they dealt with thousands of fluorescent light bulbs, mercury switches, thermostats, fire extinguishers, PCB ballasts, and other chemical containers and oils. By efficiently dealing with the site, DEP and EPA made it possible for Brewer to move along with planning for the site and complete the redevelopment quickly.

The Maine DEP's aggressive attention to environmental contamination was an essential ingredient in the success of this project. It was that initial state involvement that eventually led to further state and federal support for the project (see Figures 5.18 and 5.19).

Figure 5.18. Site before redevelopment, 2007 (photo courtesy of the Cianbro Corporation).

Figure 5.19. Site after redevelopment, 2008 (photo courtesy of the Cianbro Corporation).

While the immediate cleanup of the site was crucial in regaining jobs and economic investment in the community, it was also important in terms of the surrounding properties. The area surrounding Eastern Fine Paper had many other industrial sites, including machine shops, a former automobile and battery recycler, a boatyard and boat maintenance facility, and several former bulk petroleum-storage facilities. Over the four years that the site was closed, the waterfront area lost a number of these businesses, creating additional brownfields. Fortunately, because of the city's success with Eastern Fine Paper, they have halted some of this decline and are prepared to deal with the issues facing the surrounding areas. The success of the cleanup has given the city and SBR the experience to continue cleaning up and redeveloping the waterfront.

In order to meet the short time frame of the project, a cooperative and innovative cleanup technique was employed, which involved combining the remediation and site work into one simultaneous process. This was done with the help from the EPA, Maine DEP, and the Cianbro Corporation. Many of the contaminated soils on-site had to be remediated through on-site capping. Therefore, surface materials were chosen to meet both the requirements of the central pad and also equipment and supply storage areas, as well as the specifications for the capping material. The use of the various EPA-funded Brownfields Cleanup Grants and Revolving Loan Funding also allowed the remediation and site work to be completed simultaneously and successfully.

LAND-USE AND DESIGN CONSIDERATIONS

The redevelopment of the Eastern Fine Paper site was centered on the need for revitalization and job development. The community of Brewer was fortunate that Cianbro accomplished both of these goals as they remediated and redeveloped the site. Initially, when Eastern Fine Paper closed, the city had imagined the site being redeveloped for mixed use. This would have been much more difficult to develop at the time. By finding one company that would be able to utilize the whole site, Brewer saw an immediate increase in employment and a revitalization of the waterfront and adjacent businesses. Not only was it unique that industry could be brought back to the site so quickly, but that the layout and design of the site would be such a good fit. Cianbro needed a large space for building their modules, as well as access to the water for their shipping. The site's characteristics were a perfect fit, which meant that once the cleanup was complete the design for the site was fairly straightforward. The majority of the site's structures were torn down, while a few were restored to serve the needs of the company. The dock was built to meet their shipping requirements, and the remainder of the site was capped and laid out for material storage, production, and assembly (see Figures 5.20 and 5.21).

Being located at the waterfront presented several key design challenges. The entire site had to be regraded to accommodate the 400-foot-long barges that Cianbro needed, and this regrading resulted in a completed flat site, well suited for ship access. The location along the water made the site appealing for sturgeon fish that used the location as breeding grounds. This required extensive review and consultation between the project developers and the state fish and wildlife agency. A Revolutionary War–era shipwreck lay buried deep below the water next to the site, and only after extensive archeological investigation was the Cianbro Corporation given the authority to use the waterway as a shipping channel—with the one condition that they not disturb the shipwreck while conducting route dredging.

Figure 5.20. Site before redevelopment, 2007 (photo courtesy of the Cianbro Corporation).

Figure 5.21. Site after redevelopment, 2008 (photo courtesy of the Cianbro Corporation).

ECONOMICS

In 2004 almost 5 percent of Brewer's population lost their jobs due to the closing of Eastern Fine Paper.[8] For ninety years the company was the city's largest employer and largest taxpayer. In the four years following the mill's closure, the city of Brewer faced an increase in joblessness, a decrease in home values, and a growing number of brownfields. While taxes and water rates increased, the tax base decreased. The former paper mill was in a neighborhood where 26 percent of households were earning less than $15,000 per year.[9]

However, with the opening of the Cianbro facility, the city has seen positive change. Over 500 jobs have been created, and the community is extremely happy with the results. "A city resident, who worked at the mill for 17 years, also is happy about the new jobs, especially since he's one of the hundreds working for Cianbro. 'I didn't think I'd be back here,' he said with a big smile on his face."[10]

Another important factor in the Cianbro project has been the city's concerted effort to see the project through successfully. Completing the project in four years was an unprecedented feat made possible by the city's focused determination. In an interview, D'arcy Main-Boyington, the managing director of SBR, said, "We had to be creative with this project. We knew we had to control our destiny and we weren't going to take 'no' for an answer. The site was just too important to our community. We knocked on everyone's doors and our funders saw our commitment to the project. We were united throughout the whole process."[11]

Through these efforts the city was able to leverage funding from many different sources, including the EPA ($350,000 in grants, $1.5 million in loans), the state ($2 million in grants), and federal transportation earmarks ($3.55 million in grants). The transportation earmarks were used to fund entrance and shoreline improvements for the site. Additionally, the city established a tax-increment-financing (TIF) district at the site to raise funding to support the provision of additional infrastructure. This success with their first brownfield project has given Brewer city leaders the confidence that they will be able to continue this work successfully throughout their community.

COMMUNITY

Today Maine's economy struggles with the loss of many of its desirable manufacturing jobs; however, much of the highly skilled workforce still remains. The redevelopment of the site in Brewer was about the well-being of the city's residents. The city knew that they had to create opportunities for their workforce, and the Cianbro Corporation made that a reality. Public outreach efforts for the project were quite limited; the top-down nature of the project provided little room for community input.

Although the community is still challenged with poverty and blight around the waterfront, the redevelopment serves as a catalyst for reversing the blight in the area, reducing the risk of hazardous contaminants, and diminishing the stigma that has affected property values. City officials have worked hard to communicate their successes through local media outlets and their website, where they have touted winning a U.S. EPA Phoenix award for excellence in brownfields reuse.

CURRENT STATUS

Today the city of Brewer is looking to continue the redevelopment of their waterfront and the sites surrounding the Eastern Manufacturing Facility (see Figures 5.22 and 5.23). They hope to incorporate a waterfront trail and additional green space as part of their plan to become a high-tech, cultural, and retail center. It is their hope that their success can serve as an example and that it will help other small towns and cities to find ways to redevelop their aging industrial sites and brownfields.

LESSONS LEARNED

Throughout this project, the Brewer city officials surrounded themselves with the best team possible. The individuals working on the redevelopment were not afraid to ask questions, and through networking they were able to learn a great deal from other groups that were working on other brownfield redevelopment projects. SBR's director reached out to other communities in Maine and ended up creating a collaborative net-

Figure 5.22. Site before redevelopment, 2007 (photo courtesy of the Cianbro Corporation).

Figure 5.23. Site after redevelopment, 2008 (photo courtesy of the Cianbro Corporation).

work of professionals. She believes that it was through this outreach and SBR's willingness to ask questions that made the project go as smoothly as it did. With determination, creativity, and experienced advisors, South Brewer Redevelopment, LLC, was able to accomplish their goals and feel prepared to begin other similar projects in their city.

THE WATERSHED AT HILLSDALE, PORTLAND, OREGON

Watershed: that area of land, a bounded hydrologic system, within which all living things are inextricably linked by their common water course and where, as humans settled, simple logic demanded that they become part of a community.[12]

PROJECT BACKGROUND

The Watershed is a mixed-use, transit-oriented, green development in the heart of the Hillsdale town center in southwest Portland, Oregon. The

---

BOX 5.9

The Watershed at Hillsdale

Location:	Southwest Capitol Highway, Portland, Oregon
Site size:	0.6 acres
Owner:	Community Partners for Affordable Housing Inc. (CPAH)
Former Use:	Hay barn, rail stop, auto wrecking and fueling, storage
Current Use:	Mixed use—housing, commercial and office space, community center
Contaminant(s):	Petroleum-contaminated soil
Team:	Executive Director—Community Partnership for Affordable Housing
	Project Manager—Housing Development Center
	Architect—William Wilson Architects
	Construction Manager—Walsh Construction
	Environmental Engineer—Hahn and Associates
	President—Hillsdale Neighborhood Association
Total Cost of Project:	$11,671,720
Website:	http://www.cpahinc.org/watershed.html

BOX 5.10
_____

TIMELINE

1900–1950s Fulton Park Dairy (hay barn on southern portion).

1920s Bertha Station—stop on interurban rail.

1930–1940s Auto-wrecking and fueling facility.

1957 Site purchased by Oregon Department of Transportation (ODOT).

1990s Site used by ODOT for paper-recycling storage and over-night vehicle storage.

1998 Site considered for Multnomah County Library, but not pursued because of unknown contamination.

2001 CPAH begins planning for redevelopment.

2008 Project completed.

---

project, with its two- and three-story buildings attached by a glass sky bridge, includes commercial condos, office space, and senior housing (see Figure 5.24). The Watershed was designed to reduce its impact on the environment and to contribute to the strong identity and economic vitality of the Hillsdale town center. The neighborhood recognized the need for additional senior housing, but also faced a shortage of buildable land. By reclaiming a vacant and underutilized parcel, Community Partners for Affordable Housing (CPAH) was able to satisfy this need and enhance the entrance to the town center (see Figure 5.25).

The project team was headed by a project manager at the nonprofit Housing Development Center along with the executive director of the Community Partners for Affordable Housing. The two project leaders worked in close collaboration with environmental engineers, architects, construction managers, and the president of the Hillsdale Neighborhood Association to shepherd the project from conception to completion.

Developed with strong support from the local community, the project includes 51 units of housing for seniors, 40 of which serve low-income residents. Eight of the apartments provide supportive housing for homeless veterans who receive services from the nearby Veteran's

Figure 5.24. The Watershed completed, with sky bridge and plaza, 2008 (photo courtesy of Sally Painter).

Administration staff. The development also includes a 2,000-square-foot community center that can be used for meetings, social events, and other gatherings. The 3,200 square feet of commercial and office space is located on the ground floor of the building. All parking for the building is located in an underground garage. The Watershed project incorporates several innovative green-building techniques and building materials that minimize life-cycle costs. The project is expected to receive Leadership in Energy and Environmental Design (LEED) Silver rating.

SITE HISTORY

The small site has been used for a number of purposes over the last hundred years. From the early twentieth century to the 1950s, a portion of the site was used for a hay barn. During the 1920s it served as a stop on the interurban rail. From the 1930s to the 1940s it was used for an auto-wrecking and fueling facility. In 1957 the site was purchased by the Oregon Department of Transportation (ODOT). In the 1990s the ODOT used the site for recycling storage and overnight vehicle storage. As developable land became scarce, the site was considered for other projects. The

Figure 5.25. Site before remediation and development, 2006 (photo courtesy of Craig Kelley, Housing Development Center).

surrounding Multnomah County considered the site for a library branch but did not pursue the project because of unknown contamination. It wasn't until 2001 that the future of the site became known. CPAH saw the site as a promising opportunity for the community and overcame its constraints to succeed in creating a valuable community resource.

ENVIRONMENTAL CONSIDERATIONS

The project's site presented initial complications to redevelopment. To begin with, the site is triangular. It is surrounded by three roads and had a fifteen-foot grade change (see Figure 5.26). Initially, the geotechnical investigation of the site showed that there was both contaminated soil and nonstructural fill. During its prior use as a gasoline filling station, several spills resulted in petroleum contamination in the soil. CPAH was unable to do a full investigation until they owned the site. Once they did, the full geotechnical report revealed native soils that were prone to liquefaction during an earthquake. Because of this condition, they were required to use deep

Figure 5.26. Site during remediation and construction, 2006 (photo courtesy of Community Partners for Affordable Housing).

pilings instead of geopiers. Their plans also included insulated concrete forms (ICFs) and stored rainwater. Because these both increased weight loads, the piling and grade beam costs were increased significantly.

Although faced with these multiple site challenges, the Watershed project has successfully incorporated numerous green building techniques and sustainable development features. Innovations include a high-efficiency central hot-water boiler, durable building envelope materials, highly efficient energy-conserving windows, and an innovative heat-recovering ventilation system. Storm water will be detained on-site and will be naturally pretreated with rain gardens to help maintain water quality in the surrounding Stephens Creek and Fanno Creek watersheds. By locating all of the project's parking underground they've reduced the urban heat-island effect and allowed for a more pedestrian-friendly experience in the Hillsdale town center.

Using these techniques, the project has been able to decrease their energy and water consumption to 30 percent lower than the state of Oregon requires. They've increased the building durability, lowered the maintenance and operating costs, and improved the indoor environmental air quality. The project serves as a successful example of a dense (85 units/ acre) transit-oriented development. Not only has the project met the community's goals for creating a green building that protects the local hydrology, but it has also created a gateway to the Hillsdale town center.

LAND USE AND DESIGN CONSIDERATIONS

As discussed above, the site of the Watershed had both benefits and drawbacks. The vicinity to the center of town allowed the designers to showcase the building as the entrance to Hillsdale. However, the size, shape, and grading of the site presented some initial complications for the project. "Given the size and constraints of the site, we knew . . . we'd need to build small units and limited parking. This made a senior housing project the best alternative," said Sheila Greenlaw-Fink, the executive director of CPAH. "Given its location with shopping and services within walking distance, it seemed ideal for seniors, many of whom desire to be car-free."[13] By building the parking underground, although more costly than surface-level parking, CPAH was also able to maximize the buildable space on the site (see Figure 5.27). They could incorporate components to the building that the community expressed a need for, such as the community center.

Figure 5.27. Site during construction, 2007 (photo courtesy of Craig Kelley, Housing Development Center).

The community and future residents were included and considered a priority throughout the design process. CPAH hired a nationally known senior-housing specialist to advise them on the design of the building. Acknowledging the visual and social needs of the aging residents, the building reflects conscious decisions in lighting design, color selection, unit layout, and common area design. The complex is well designed for its residents, but most important it has also become a part of greater Hillsdale. Purchased with funds raised by the community, the complex includes a large illuminated sign that reads "Hillsdale" rather than "The Watershed." The project is not just an affordable housing project—it is a shared part of the community.

ECONOMICS

The Watershed was a complicated project, but rather then looking at their challenges as barriers, project planners saw them as opportunities for funding. Overall, the project budget came to over $11 million. Fifty-nine percent of the project was financed through Low-Income Housing tax credits. The remaining funding came from a variety of sources. Twenty-four percent of this remaining funding came from loans, to be repaid through revenues from market-rate office and residential leases at the site. Seven percent came from what the project called "Brown to Green" sources, which included agencies such as the EPA and numerous local organizations. Three percent came from housing grants and the last 8 percent came from the sale of the commercial condo unit and commercial and housing funds. By combining the brownfield cleanup, affordable housing, and green design, the project was able to successfully leverage a variety of funding sources.

COMMUNITY

The community was intricately involved in the Watershed project. From the beginning, CPAH held community design charettes to get input from the neighborhood residents and businesses. Originally, the project was to be named Bertha Station, but the community felt the project deserved a more meaningful name. They chose Watershed because the site is between the Tualatin and Willamette River watersheds, and it's also at the headwaters of Stephens and Fanno Creeks. They thought the name was also useful in representing the green aspect of the project and the fact that it is sensitively handling all the storm water it can on-site. Finally, they felt the project represented a "watershed moment" in their development history, as the site was one of the last pieces of buildable land in their neighborhood.

In addition to design input and charette participation, local neighborhood and business associations helped with the funding process and raised their own funds to pay for the lighting of the Hillsdale sign and tower as well as a public water fountain (see Figure 5.28). Overall, the

Figure 5.28. The Watershed completed, Hillsdale tower, 2008 (photo courtesy of Sally Painter).

community played a vital role throughout every stage of the project. The importance of ongoing, sustained community involvement was one of the most important lessons learned during the project.

LESSONS LEARNED

Being CPAH's first brownfield redevelopment, there were many lessons learned throughout each stage of the project. The first such lesson was the importance of team building. From the start, CPAH made sure that everyone involved in the project was on board and committed to the project goals. Using a visual project roadmap, the members of the project team were able to see what their own roles were and who was responsible for the different steps. Creativity and flexibility is always necessary for these types of projects, and CPAH made sure that all of their team members were willing to think outside the box and challenge themselves to complete the project successfully.

The local community was included in the project planning from the beginning. Not only were they informed, but they were also listened to and included in the designs. By including the community from the start they found people were more excited about the project and less hesitant about the remediation. Bringing local businesses and neighborhood associations on board provided willing recipients for brownfield information, and through these groups the information was spread throughout the community. They also recognized that the experts from the EPA and other agencies could help to reduce perceived risks in the community.

After completing the project, CPAH realized that most affordable-housing projects deal with some level of contamination or perceived risk. Having such a positive experience redeveloping their first brownfield site, CPAH saw that brownfield cleanups could become a niche for them and that they could help other nonprofits do similar work. While they have not begun another brownfield redevelopment, CPAH is excited about future prospective projects.

CURRENT STATUS

The Watershed was completed in February 2008. Today the development serves as the gateway into the Hillsdale community and as an ideal place

for its senior residents to live. At the time of this writing, the senior housing is fully occupied and the commercial space is fully leased out. The
building offers a roof deck for gardening, lobbies for social gatherings,
conference rooms for events, and a plaza open to the public. The project
continues to foster community and support the emotional health of its
residents.

ADDITIONAL RESOURCES

Bhandari, Alok, Rao Y. Surampalli, Pascale Champagne, and Say Kee Ong, eds. 2007. *Remediation technologies for soils and groundwater.* Reston, VA: American Society of Civil Engineers.

The Brownfields and Land Revitalization Technology Support Center, www .brownfieldstsc.org/

BLRTSC, formerly the Brownfields Technology Support Center, is a cooperative effort to provide technical support and answers to federal, state, local, and tribal officials for questions related to the use of innovative technologies and strategies for site assessment and cleanup.

Davis, Todd. 2002. *Brownfields: A comprehensive guide to redeveloping contaminated property.* Chicago: American Bar Association Publishing.

De Sousa, Christopher. 2008. *Brownfields redevelopment and the quest for sustainability.* Current issues in urban and regional studies series, vol. 3. London: Elsevier Science / Emerald Group Publishing.

Dixon, Tim, David Lerner, Mike Raco, and Philip Catney, eds. 2007. *Sustainable brownfield regeneration: Liveable places from problem spaces.* Malden, MA: Wiley-Blackwell.

Environmental Protection Agency's Brownfields Office, www.epa.gov/brown fields

Eslinger, Eric. 1994. *Introduction to environmental hydrogeology: With emphasis on evaluation and remediation of hydrocarbon contamination in groundwater and soil.* Tulsa, OK: SEPM (Society for Sedimentary Geology).

Greenstein, Roz, and Yesim Sungu-Eryilmaz, eds. 2004. *Recycling the city: The use and reuse of urban land.* Cambridge, MA: Lincoln Institute of Land Policy.

Gute, David, and Michael Taylor. 2006. Revitalizing neighborhoods through sustainable brownfields redevelopment: Principles put into practice in Bridgeport, CT. Local Environment 11 (5):537–58.

Jackson-Elmoore, Cynthia, Richard Hula, and Laura Reese, eds. 2010. Environmental contamination, adaptive reuse, and public health. Lansing: Michigan State University Press.

Kirkwood, Niall, ed. 2001. Manufactured sites: rethinking the post-industrial landscape. Oxford: Taylor and Francis.

The National Brownfield Association, www.brownfieldassociation.org

A Chicago-based, nonprofit, member-based organization dedicated to promoting the sustainable development of brownfields.

National Center for Neighborhood and Brownfields Redevelopment, www.policy .rutgers.edu/brownfields/

A national center focused on themes of service and research for the promotion of neighborhood and brownfields redevelopment based at the Rutgers University's E. J. Bloustein School of Planning & Public Policy.

National Vacant Properties Campaign, www.vacantproperties.org/index.html

The Northeast-Midwest Institute, www.nemw.org/

A Washington-based, private, nonprofit, and nonpartisan research organization dedicated to economic vitality, environmental quality, and regional equity for states in the Northeast and Midwest.

Pendergrass, John. 2000. Sustainable redevelopment of brownfields: Using institutional controls to protect public health. Environmental Law Reporter 29:10243.

Powers, C., F. Hoffman, D. Brown, and C. Conner. 2000. Experiment: Brownfields pilots catalyze revitalization. New Brunswick, NJ: Institute for Responsible Management Inc.

Russ, Thomas. 1999. Redeveloping brownfields: Landscape architects, site planners, developers. New York: McGraw-Hill.

Simons, Robert A. 2006. When bad things happen to good property. Washington, DC: Environmental Law Institute.

Solitare, Laura. 2005. Prerequisite conditions for meaningful participation in brownfields redevelopment. Journal of Environmental Planning and Management 48 (6):917–35.

West Virginia Brownfields Assistance Center, www.wvbrownfields.com
An effort to encourage, promote, and publicize the development of brownfields
   into viable real estate.
Western Pennsylvania Brownfields Center at Carnegie Mellon University, www
   .cmu.edu/steinbrenner/brownfields/index.html

NOTES

CHAPTER 1:

1. Bartsch, C., and E. Collaton, *Brownfields: Cleaning and Reusing Contaminated Properties* (Westport, CT: Praeger, 1997); Greenberg, Michael R., Frank J. Popper, and Bernadette West, "The TOADS: A New American Urban Experience," *Urban Affairs Quarterly* 25, no. 3 (1990):435–54; Yount, Kristen R., and Peter B. Meyer, "Bankers, Developers, and New Investment in Brownfields Sites: Environmental Concerns and the Social Psychology of Risk," *Economic Development Quarterly* 8, no. 4 (1994):338–44.

2. Other nations define brownfields as property that is idle, but previously developed, without respect to contamination.

3. Bartsch and Collaton, *Brownfields* (see chap. 1, n. 1); De Sousa, Christopher A., "Measuring the Public Costs and Benefits of Brownfield versus Greenfield Development in the Greater Toronto Area," *Environment and Planning B: Planning and Design* 29, no. 2 (2002):251–80; De Sousa, Christopher A., "Unearthing the Benefits of Brownfield to Greenspace Projects: An Examination of Project Use and Quality of Life Impacts, *Local Environment: The International Journal of Justice and Sustainability* 11, no. 5 (2006):577–600; Hollander, Justin B., *Polluted, and Dangerous: America's Worst Abandoned Properties and What can Be Done about Them* (Burlington, VT: University of Vermont Press, 2009); Simons, Robert, "How Many Brownfields Are Out There? An Economic Base Contraction Analysis of 31 U.S. Cities, *Public Works Management and Policy* 2, no. 3

(1999):267–73; Simons, Robert A., *When Bad Things Happen to Good Property* (Washington, DC: Environmental Law Institute, 2006).

4. Environmental justice is the pursuit of the fair and equitable distribution of environmental benefits and harms, both spatially and among different races and classes; cf. Agyeman, Julian, *Sustainable Communities and the Challenge of Environmental Justice* (New York: New York University Press, 2005); Bullard, Robert D., *Dumping in Dixie: Race, Class, and Environmental Quality* (Boulder, CO: Westview Press, 2000); Schlosberg, David, *Defining Environmental Justice: Theories, Movements, and Nature* (Oxford: Oxford University Press, 2007).

5. Greenberg, Michael R., Diane Downton, and Henry Mayer, "Are Mothballed Brownfields Sites a Major Problem?" *Public Management* 85, no. 5 (2003):12–17.

6. Gonzalez, George A., *Urban Sprawl, Global Warming, and the Empire of Capital* (Albany, NY: SUNY Press, 2009).

7. Simons, "How Many Brownfields Are Out There?" (see chap. 1, n. 3).

8. Known as High-Impact Temporarily Obsolete Abandoned Derelict Sites (HI-TOADS); see Greenberg, Michael R., Karen Lowrie, Laura Solitare, and Latoya Duncan, "Brownfields, TOADS, and the Struggle for Neighborhood Redevelopment: A Case Study of New Jersey, *Urban Affairs Review* 35, no. 5 (2000):717–33; also Hollander, *Polluted, and Dangerous* (see chap. 1, n. 3).

9. Greenberg, Michael R., and Justin B. Hollander, "The EPA's Brownfields Pilot Program: A Multi–Geographically Layered and Socially Desirable Innovation," *American Journal of Public Health* 96, no. 2 (2006):277–81.

CHAPTER 2

1. The EPA is involved in brownfields where the site has been placed on the National Priority List under the Superfund program or where the level or nature of contamination is beyond the technical capabilities of state regulators (e.g., some types of nuclear contamination).

2. Greenberg and Hollander. "The EPA's Brownfields Pilot Program" (see chap. 1, n. 9); Greenberg, Michael R., and Laura Solitare, "Is the U.S. Environmental Protection Agency Brownfield Assessment Pilot Program Environmentally Just?" *Environmental Health Perspectives* 110, suppl. 2 (2002):249–57.

3. Bartsch and Collaton, *Brownfields* (see chap. 1, n. 1).

4. U.S. Environmental Protection Agency, *Partnership for Sustainable Communities* website, 2009, http://www.epa.gov/opei/ocmp/dced-partnership.html (accessed June 19, 2009).

5. For details on the kinds of programs and policies states have adopted, see Meyer, Peter B., and Kristen R. Yount, "Financing Redevelopment of Brown-

fields," in White, Sammis B., Richard D. Bingham, and Edward W. Hill, eds., *Financing Economic Development in the 21st Century* (Armonk, NY: M. E. Sharpe, 2003); see also the EPA's semi-regular report: U.S. Environmental Protection Agency, *State Brownfields and Voluntary Response Programs: An Update from the States*, 2008, EPA-560-R-08-004, http://epa.gov/brownfields/pubs/st_res _prog_report.htm (accessed June 19, 2009).

6. To learn if you are in a state with LSPs, contact the National Association of Environmental Professionals <www.naep.org>.

7. Meyer and Yount, "Financing redevelopment of brownfields" (see chap. 2, n. 5).

8. For a discussion about how TIF was used in two cases in Minnesota, see Zachman, Jeff, and Susan D. Steinwell, "The Use of TIF in Redeveloping Brownfields in Minnesota," in Johnson, Craig L., and Joyce Y. Man, eds., *Tax Increment Financing and Economic Development: Uses, Structure, and Impact* (Albany, NY: State University of New York Press, 2001).

9. The Comprehensive Environmental Response, Compensation, and Liability Act ("CERCLA"), is also known as the Federal Superfund Act. CERCLA was substantially amended by the Superfund Amendments and Reauthorization Act (SARA) on October 17, 1986.

10. The Small Business Liability Relief and Brownfields Revitalization Act ("Amendment") was signed into law on January 11, 2002.

CHAPTER 5

1. One of the authors (Julia Gold) worked as an employee of The Steel Yard in 2007, and she currently resides in a building adjacent to the site.

2. Interview with Drake Patten, conducted by Julia Gold on January 22, 2009.

3. Interview with Leah Yasenchak, conducted March 4, 2009, by Julia Gold.

4. While the project used a number of environmentally sound practices, the developers did not seek out Leadership in Energy and Environmental Design (LEED) certification.

5. Dispenza, Kristin, "Cargo Shipping Containers Are an International Salvage Resource," posted on GreenBuildingElements.com, July 22, 2008, http://greenbuildingelements.com/2008/07/22/cargo-shipping-containers-are-an-international-salvage-resource/ (accessed February 24, 2009).

6. "African American group plans green community center on old brownfield," *The Sentinel* (Portland, OR), Janurary 6, 2010, http://www.portlandsentinel .com/node/5694 (accessed February 19, 2010).

7. Interview with Chris Poole-Jones, conducted February 26, 2009, by Julia Gold.

8. U.S. Environmental Protection Agency, "Former Mill Redeveloped to Create 500 Jobs," posted 2008, http://www.epa.gov/brownfields/success/brewer_me_ss.pdf (accessed February 19, 2010).

9. U.S. Environmental Protection Agency, "Brownfields 2006 Grant Fact Sheet, South Brewer Redevelopment LLC, Brewer, ME" (Washington, DC: U.S. EPA, 2006).

10. Ricker, Nok-Noi, "Workers Celebrated at Cianbro Opening," *Bangor Daily News* (Bangor, ME), August 16, 2008, http://www.brewerme.org/Cianbro/cianbro_eastern_manufacturing_workers.htm (accessed February 3, 2008).

11. Interview with D'arcy Main Boyington, conducted February 2, 2009, by Julia Gold.

12. Fink, Sheila, and Craig Kelley, "From BROWN to GREEN: The Watershed @ Hillsdale Senior Housing," Powerpoint Presentation for Metro Brownfield Workshop, May 31, 2007.

13. Lotts, Karen, 2008. "The Watershed—Low-Income Housing with a Green Personality," *The Times* (Tigard, OR), January 31, 2008, http://www.tigardtimes.com/sustainable/story_2nd.php?story_id=120174451836798600 (accessed February 20, 2010).

INDEX

Page numbers followed by an "f" indicate figures/photos/illustrations.

Activity Use Limitation (AUL), 17, 55–56, 60–61
agency(ies), 9, 94, 118. *See also specific agencies*
  approval by, 22
  fish and wildlife, 105
  municipal, 80–81
  Rhode Island state, 78
  state/local, 10
agriculture, 23, 55
air, 3, 24, 27, 36, 114
  sparging, 31
analysis, 40, 43, 48
  sampling, 45, 49f
  site, 21, 24
archeology, 105
arts, 68, 73, 74, 77, 82
Assunpink Greenway Project, Trenton, New Jersey, 11, 66
  challenges for, 89–90
  community and, 88–89
  Crescent Wire site of, 83f, 84f
  current status of, 89
  environmental considerations of, 84–85
  funding, 87–88, 89
  goals, 87
  land use/design, 86–87
  project background, 80–83
  site, 85f, 86f

site history, 83–84
site plan, 82f
timeline, 81
website, 80
attenuation, natural, 34, 40
AUL. *See* Activity Use Limitation

bacteria, 31, 32
barrier
  geo membrane, 72
  permeable reactive, 34
  waterproof, 62
Bauta, Nick, 69, 75
biodegradation, 31, 32, 34
biofuel, 55
bioremediation, 31–32, 33, 39
bioswales, 72, 75, 95
bioventing, 32
Boston, Massachusetts, 53f
"brightfields" programs, 55
Brown University, 69
brownfield(s), 1
  classes of, 5
  elements of, site, 23–24
  EPA, program, 13
  examples of, 2
  federal, programs, 12–13, 96
  local, coordinator, 18
  number/location of, 4–5
  restrictions on, end use, 17, 56
  settings of, 23

129

brownfield(s) (*continued*)
  site in Chelsea, Massachusetts, 5f
  state, programs, 13–15, 55
  typical, pollution, 27–30
building(s), 24, 25, 50
  green, 62, 66, 92, 94, 96, 97, 112, 114, 115,
    116, 117
  reuse of, 52, 58, 60

capping, 39, 56, 57, 60, 62, 72–73, 74, 104, 105
carbon footprint, 3, 4, 73
carcinogens, 28, 29
CDBG. *See* Community Development Block
    Grant
CERCLA, 16
challenges, 65
  for Assunpink Greenway, 89–90
  for Eastern Manufacturing Facility, 108–109
  for June Key Community Center Demon-
    stration Project, 97
  for The Steel Yard, 77–79
  for The Watershed, 113–114, 116, 118
Chelsea, Massachusetts, brownfield site in, 5f
Cianbro Corporation, 98–99, 101, 104, 106,
    107
  site, 100f
cleanup, 1, 8, 65, 76, 100. *See also* remediation
    , 37, 38
  innovative, 104
  methods, 21
  nonintrusive, 37, 40
  partial in-place, 37, 39
  partial off-site, 37, 38–39
  standards, 21
community, 3, 6, 13, 37, 48, 52
  Assunpink and, 88–89
  Eastern Manufacturing Facility and, 107
  June Key Community Center Demonstra-
    tion Project and, 95, 96
  outreach, 8, 11–12, 57, 58, 65, 66, 95
  service, 91, 92
  The Steel Yard and, 76
  The Watershed and, 111, 116–118, 119
Community Development Block Grant
    (CDBG), 13
Community Partners for Affordable Housing
    Inc. (CPAH), 110, 111, 113, 115, 116, 118
concealment, full, 37, 39–40
contamination, 1, 5, 16, 17, 19, 42, 68, 80, 98,
    101, 107, 110, 113, 118. *See also* pollution
  areas of, 24–25
  evaluation of, levels, 40–41
  ground water, 26, 62
  lead, at The Steel Yard, 71, 72f

levels, 14, 22, 23–25, 37, 43, 44–48
  maximum detectable limits of, 21
  on-site containment of, 74
  of sediments, 26–27
  soil, 25–26, 33, 56, 60
  spread of, 39
  subsurface, plumes, 25
  surface water, 26, 85, 86
cost, 15, 16, 17, 31, 37, 38, 48, 68, 80, 91, 98,
    110
  reduction, 14, 43, 76, 114
CPAH. *See* Community Partners for Afford-
    able Housing Inc.
cultural activities, 52, 56, 63, 73

degradation, 29, 34, 35
Delta Sigma Theta Sorority Inc., 66, 91, 93,
    95, 96. *See also* June Key Community
    Center Demonstration Project, Port-
    land, Oregon
demolition, 50, 53, 61
Department of Energy (DOE), 13
  "brightfields" programs, 55
Department of Housing and Urban Develop-
    ment (HUD), 13
design, 6, 8, 56, 69, 112
  green, 96, 116
  land use and, 51, 60–61, 73–75, 86–87, 95,
    104–105, 115–116
  phases, 54
  remediation process and, 57, 58–59
designer, 62
  flexibility of, 56
  role of, 56–60, 63
dewatering, 38
documents, 41, 48, 49
DOE. *See* Department of Energy
drainage, site, 62–63
dredging, 50, 105

East Trenton Collaborative, 88–89
Eastern Fine Paper Company, 98, 100, 101f
  remediation, 101–103
Eastern Manufacturing Facility, Brewer,
    Maine, 66
  challenges for, 108–109
  community and, 107
  current status of, 108
  economics and, 106–107
  environmental considerations, 101–104
  funding, 107
  land use/design and, 104–105
  project background, 98–99
  site, 102f, 103f, 105f, 106f, 108f, 109f

site history, 99–101
timeline, 99, 104, 107
website, 98
ecology, 56, 63
Economic Development Administration
(EDA), 13
economy, 4, 13, 56, 57, 75, 81, 103
Eastern Manufacturing Facility and, 106–
107
EDA. *See* Economic Development
Administration
education, 60, 73, 77, 82, 94
environmental, 73, 95, 97
employment, 58, 100, 103, 104, 106
encapsulation, 32, 39, 46f, 47
end use, 22. *See also* Activity Use Limitation
(AUL)
restrictions on brownfield, 17, 56
energy, 4, 44, 112
consumption, 114
efficiency, 3
renewable/alternative, 55, 73, 95
environment, 3, 12, 14, 15, 19, 21, 57, 112. *See
also* site assessment
Assunpink Greenway and, 84–86
Eastern Manufacturing Facility and, 101–
104
education about, 73, 95, 97
June Key Community Center Demonstration Project and, 94–95
protection of, 1, 17
The Steel Yard and, 71–73
The Watershed and, 113–115
environmental consultants, 14, 40, 50
environmental engineers, 21, 40, 41, 43, 48,
49, 50, 57, 58, 78, 111
Environmental Protection Agency (EPA), 1,
10, 12, 75, 96, 100, 101–102, 104, 118
Brownfields Program, 13
Phoenix award, 107
websites, 13, 17
EPA. *See* Environmental Protection Agency
equipment, 37, 38, 39, 50, 57, 104
excavation, 33, 38, 50, 62
sub-grade, 57
experience, 7, 10, 104, 109

flexibility, 8, 56, 90, 118
flooding, 66, 81, 82–83, 85
funding, 8, 12, 13, 16, 73
Assunpink Greenway, 87–88, 89
Eastern Manufacturing Facility, 107
June Key Community Center Demonstration Project, 95–96

revolving loan, 104
The Steel Yard, 75–76
The Watershed, 116, 117
fungi, 31

gardens, 55, 61, 95, 119
rain, 72, 75, 114
storm-water, 62
gas station, 5, 38, 91, 95, 113
gases, 27, 36, 44
gasoline, 28, 44
geo membrane barrier, 72
geology, 14, 39, 40
geophysical technology, 40, 47
GPR. *See* ground penetrating radar
grants, 13, 75, 84, 88, 95, 96, 97, 104, 116
green building, 62, 66, 92, 94, 96, 97, 112, 114,
115, 116, 117
greenfields, preserving, 2–3, 4
Greenlaw-Fink, Sheila, 115
ground penetrating radar (GPR), 47
ground water, 22, 24, 42, 45, 46, 57
contamination, 26, 62
treatment, 31–32, 34–35, 38, 58

health, 17, 21, 28, 29–30, 42, 58, 85
herbicides, 28
historical sites, 82
history, 82
Assunpink Greenway site, 83–84
of disposal, 44
Eastern Manufacturing Facility site, 99–101
June Key Community Center Demonstration Project site, 93–94
restoration and, 57, 60
site, 40, 42, 66
The Steel Yard site, 69–71
The Watershed site, 112–113
housing, 13, 52, 55, 60, 92, 118. *See also* Community Partners for Affordable Housing
Inc. (CPAH)
senior, 111, 115, 116, 119
HUD. *See* Department of Housing and Urban
Development
hydrogeology, 14, 40, 42, 44, 46

ICFs. *See* insulated concrete forms
immunoassays, 44
incineration, 33
industrial waste, 24, 25, 40, 41, 43
infiltration, 86, 87
infrastructure, 2, 16, 27, 50, 52, 58, 60, 107
above/below ground, 24
living, 62

insects, 24
insulated concrete forms (ICFs), 114
insurance, 8, 12, 17–18
    website regarding, 17

June Key Community Center Demonstration
    Project, Portland, Oregon
    challenges for, 97
    community and, 95, 96
    current status, 97
    environmental considerations of, 94–95
    funding, 95–96
    goal of, 93
    land use / design and, 95
    project background, 91–92
    site before development, 93f
    site history, 93–94
    site rendering, 94f, 95, 96f
    timeline, 92
    website, 91

land farming, 33, 40
land use, 1
    design and, 51, 60–61, 73–75, 86–87, 95,
        104–105, 115–116
    of neighborhood, 52, 61
    temporary, 55–56
landfills, 2, 23, 40, 47, 51
    licensed, 33, 38, 72
laws, 17–18
    CERCLA federal, 16
lead, 30, 68
    contamination at The Steel Yard, 71, 72f
Leadership in Energy and Environmental De-
    sign (LEED), Silver rating, 112
LEED. See Leadership in Energy and Environ-
    mental Design
LEP. See licensed environmental
    professionals
liability, 6, 8
    legal, 16–17
    owner's, 4
    website regarding, 17
licensed environmental professionals (LEP),
    14, 37, 40
licensed site professionals (LSP), 14–15, 21, 23,
    40, 41, 43, 48, 49, 50, 58
liquefaction, 113
loans
    low-interest, 13
    revolving, 104
local government, 10, 15–16
Low-Income Housing, tax credits, 116
LSP. See licensed site professionals

Main-Boyington, D'arcy, 107
Maine Department of Environmental Protec-
    tion, 100, 101–102, 104
maps, 41, 42, 45
metals, 28, 29–30, 44, 68, 71, 72, 85, 98, 101
microbes, 31, 32, 34, 40
microclimate, 24, 35
monitoring wells, 46–47, 50, 57

National Oceanic and Atmospheric Agency
    (NOAA), 13
neighborhood, 8, 38, 57, 58, 59, 66, 76, 88, 97,
    103, 111
    associations, 118
    investment in, 83
    land use of, 52, 61
    quality of life for, 3
networking, 18, 108–109
NOAA. See National Oceanic and Atmo-
    spheric Agency
nonprofit(s), 11, 66, 88, 96
    status, 75
Nye, Mark, 97

oil, 2, 24, 28, 42, 43, 102
open space, 52, 54–55, 60, 82, 84

PAHs. See polycyclic aromatic hydrocarbons
parking, 25, 56, 60, 112, 114, 115
parkland, 55, 80
Partnership for Sustainable Communities, 13
Patten, Drake, 74–75, 77
PCBs. See polychlorinated biphenols
permeable reactive barrier, 34
permitting, 42, 78, 90, 97, 99
pesticides, 28
petroleum products (TPH), 28–29, 32, 44, 103,
    110, 113
phenols, 28
Phoenix award, 107
photo-ionization detectors (PID), 44
phthalates, 28
phytoremediation, 34–35, 39, 40, 72, 75
PID. See photo-ionization detectors
planning
    for remediation, 21, 48
    site, 70f, 71f, 82f
    stages, 8
    strategies, 4, 5
    urban renewal, 52
pollution, 3, 4, 16, 25, 56, 82. See also
    contamination
    range of, 22–23
    typical, on brownfield site, 27–30

polychlorinated biphenols (PCBs), 28, 29, 80, 98
polycyclic aromatic hydrocarbons (PAHs), 28, 80, 85, 101
Poole-Jones, Chris, 95, 97
poverty, 76, 83, 107
professionals, 9, 11. *See also* licensed environmental professionals (LEP); licensed site professionals (LSP)
  experienced, 10
programs, 8, 18
  DOE "brightfields," 55
  federal brownfields, 12–13, 96
  state brownfields, 13–15
project manager, 03, 75, 77, 78–79, 80, 86, 91, 95, 97, 111
property(ies), 1
  abandoned, 3
  acquisition, 84, 90
  value, 4, 83, 107
protection
  of environment, 1, 17
  of vegetation, 57
  water, 60
Providence Steel and Iron Company (PS&I), 68, 69–71
PS&I. *See* Providence Steel and Iron Company
public space, 63, 73, 82, 87
pump-and-treat systems, 35, 39, 50, 57

quality of life, 3, 63, 83

recreation, 54–55, 58, 63, 80, 82, 83, 87
recycling, 92, 94, 97
  water, 95
regulations, 1, 6, 10, 14, 30, 48, 57, 58, 86
  state/federal, 37, 50
remediation, 4, 5, 15, 18–19, 76, 99, 104, 118.
    See also bioremediation; cleanup; phytoremediation; site assessment
  assessing need for, 12, 21–30
  design and, process, 57, 58–59
  Eastern Fine Paper Company, 101–103
  emerging alternative-treatment technologies for, 31, 33, 34–35
  errors in, 16
  established treatment technologies for, 31, 32, 33, 34, 35
  implementation of, technologies, 49–50
  innovative alternative-treatment technologies for, 31–32, 34, 35–37
  organizing/assessing (Phase I- V), 37–50
  permanent, treatment, 37
  plan, 21, 48
  range of, 22

selection of, technologies, 37, 41, 48–49
  standards, 17
  strategies, 14
  supporting facilities, 37
  technologies, 6, 30–37, 75
remote sensing technology, 47
resources. *See also* programs
  federal, 66
  finding, 12–18
  natural, 3, 4
restoration, 51
  habitat, 55
  historic, 57, 60
reuse, 14, 15, 59f
  adaptive, 51, 52
  of buildings, 52, 58, 60
  commercial, 51, 54
  knowledge about, 6
  light industrial, 54
Rhode Island Department of Environmental Management (RIDEM), 71–72
Rhode Island School of Design, 69
RIDEM. *See* Rhode Island Department of Environmental Management
risk, 22, 44, 54, 107
  reduced, 118
Rockefeller, Clay, 69, 75

safety, 48
sampling, 57
  analysis, 45, 49f
SBR. *See* South Brewer Redevelopment, LLC
screening methods, 40, 43–48
sediments, 24, 45
  contamination of, 26–27
  removal of, 38
  treatment of, 34–35
semi-volatile organic compounds (SVOCs), 27–28, 98
sewerage, 54, 60, 75
site assessment, 15, 19, 24. *See also* contamination; remediation
  comprehensive, 43–48
  initial, 41, 42f, 43
soil, 22, 24, 42, 62
  chemistry, 45
  clean, coverage, 39
  contamination, 25–26, 33, 56, 60
  cut-and-fill balance of, 57
  fertility, 35
  organic, 61
  pH, 35, 45
  treatment, 31–32, 33, 34–36, 38, 58, 72
  use of, 61–62

soil flushing, 39
soil gas surveys, 44
soil vapor extraction (SVE), 36, 39
soil washing, 35–36
solidification/stabilization, 39, 72
Somerville, Massachusetts, 60–61
South Brewer Redevelopment, LLC (SBR), 98,
    100, 107, 108, 109
state
    agencies, 10, 78
    brownfield programs, 13–15, 55
    involvement, 102
    regulations, 37, 50
The Steel Yard, Providence, Rhode Island,
    65–66
    challenges for, 77–79
    community and, 76
    current status of, 76–77
    environmental considerations of, 71–73
    funding, 75–76
    land use/design, 73–75
    lead contamination at, 71, 72f
    project background, 68–69
    site, 71f
    site history, 69–71
    site plan, 70f, 71f
    site rendering, 73f, 74f, 77f
    timeline, 69
    website, 68
The Steel Yard Green Fund, 73
stigma, 3, 52, 59, 61, 107
storm-water, 84–85, 95, 114
    gardens, 62
    management, 60, 62–63, 74, 75, 87, 117
surface
    asphalt, 56
    contamination of, water, 26, 85, 86
    contamination plumes, 25
    impervious, 62
    permeable, 75, 95
sustainability, 2, 4, 6, 13, 40, 58, 59, 60, 73, 95,
    97, 114
SVE. See soil vapor extraction
SVOCs. See semi-volatile organic compounds

Tax Increment Financing, 15–16, 107
taxation, 15–16, 107, 116
team, 8, 9–11, 48, 50, 68, 80, 86, 95, 99, 108,
    111
    change in, 78
    importance of, 66, 118
technology(ies)
    emerging alternative-treatment, for reme-
        diation, 31, 33, 34–35

established treatment, for remediation, 31,
    32, 33, 34, 35
    geophysical, 40, 47
    implementation of remediation, 49–50
    innovative alternative-treatment, for reme-
        diation, 31–32, 34, 35–37
    remediation, 6, 30–37, 75
    remote sensing, 47
    selection of remediation, 37, 41, 48–49
    XRF, 44–45
thermal desorption, 36–37, 62
timeline, 8, 10, 32, 48, 61, 66, 78
    Assunpink Greenway, 81
    Eastern Manufacturing Facility, 99, 104, 107
    June Key Community Center Demonstra-
        tion Project, 92
    The Steel Yard, 69
    The Watershed, 111
topography, 24, 73
total petroleum hydrocarbons, 32. See also pe-
    troleum products (TPH)
toxicity, 28, 37
TPH. See petroleum products
transportation, 52, 54, 57, 60, 82, 107
treatment. See also technology(ies)
    ground water, 31–32, 34–35, 38, 58
    permanent remediation, 37
    of sediments, 34–35
    soil, 31–32, 33, 34–36, 38, 58, 72
    water, 58
trees, 63, 76, 82
Trenton, New Jersey, 4, 11. See also Assunpink
    Greenway Project
Triad, 14

urban renewal plans, 52
utilities, 54, 57

vapor, 27, 28, 31, 36, 39
vegetation, 24, 25, 28, 31, 44, 61, 62, 76, 82, 86
    disturbance to, 50
    integrating, 63
    living, 34, 35, 40
    native, 95
    protection of, 57
VOCs. See volatile organic compounds
volatile organic compounds (VOCs), 27–28
    detection of, 44

waste management, 26, 42, 50, 61
water, 3. See also ground water; storm-water
    bodies of, 24, 25, 50, 51
    consumption, 114
    contamination of surface, 26, 85, 86

protection, 60
quality, 83, 114
recycling, 95
removal of, bodies, 38
stored rain, 114
treatment, 58
The Watershed at Hillsdale, Portland, Oregon, 11
challenges for, 113–114, 116, 118
community and, 111, 116–118, 119
current status of, 118–119
environmental consideration and, 113–115
funding, 116, 117
land use/design, 115–116
project background, 110–112
site, 111, 112f, 113f, 114f, 115f, 117f
site history, 112–113
timeline, 111
website, 110

website(s), 18–19, 21
Assunpink Greenway, 80
Eastern Manufacturing Facility, 98
EPA, 13, 17
regarding insurance/liability, 17
June Key Community Center Demonstration Project, 91
The Steel Yard, 68
The Watershed, 110
wetlands, 55, 80, 82
wildlife, 24, 50

x-ray fluorescence (XRF) technology, 44–45
XRF. *See* x-ray fluorescence technology

Yasenchak, Leah, 80, 83, 86